HERITAGE BUILDERS

The Family Compass

This book was created as an outreach of the Heritage Builders Association—a network of families and churches committed to passing a strong heritage to the next generation. Designed to motivate and assist families as they become intentional about the heritage-passing process, these resources draw upon the collective wisdom of parents, grandparents, church leaders, and family life experts, in an effort to provide balanced, biblical parenting advice along with effective, practical tools for family living.

For more information, write, phone, or visit our Web site:

Heritage Builders Association 1-800-528-9489
c/o Chariot Victor Publishing www.chariotvictor.com
4050 Lee Vance View www.heritagebuilders.com
Colorado Springs, CO 80918

The Heritage Builders resources include:

Your Heritage
> A foundational book explaining the Heritage Builders ministry's key concepts. (Trade paper)

Family Night Tool Chest books
> *An Introduction to Family Nights* *Holidays Family Night*
> *Basic Christian Beliefs* *Simple Science*
> *Christian Character Qualities* *Money Matters for Kids*
> *Wisdom Life Skills* *Ten Commandments*
> *Bible Stories for Preschoolers (Old Testament)*
> *Bible Stories for Preschoolers (New Testament)*

Family Fragrance
> An expansion on one of the four foundational concepts of building an intentional legacy. Filled with ways to develop and create an AROMA of love in your home. (Trade paper)

Family Traditions
> One of the four foundational concepts of building an intentional legacy. Filled with ways to celebrate old traditions and mark spiritual milestones in your family. (Trade paper)

Heritage Builders Curriculum
> A small group adult study focusing on the importance of establishing and passing on a family spiritual heritage. (Thirteen-week curriculum)

These resources from Chariot Victor Publishing are available through your local Christian bookstore.

HERITAGE BUILDERS

The Family Compass

Kurt and Olivia Bruner

Chariot Victor Publishing
A Division of Cook Communications

Chariot Victor Publishing
a division of Cook Communications, Colorado Springs, Colorado 80918
Cook Communications, Paris, Ontario
Kingsway Communications, Eastbourne, England

FAMILY COMPASS
© 1999 by Kurt and Olivia Bruner. All rights reserved.

Printed in the United States of America.

1 2 3 4 5 6 7 8 9 10 Printing/Year 03 02 01 00 99

Editor: Susan Reck, Julie Smith
Interior design: Brenda Franklin
Cover design: Koechel Peterson

Library of Congress Cataloging-in-Publication Data
Bruner, Kurt D.
        Family compass/by Kurt and Olivia Bruner.
            p.   cm.
        ISBN 1-56476-781-7
        1. Child rearing--Religious aspects--Christianity. I. Bruner, Olivia.
II. Title.
BV4529.B79   1999   99-15577
248.8'45--dc21   CIP

Table of Contents

Dedication

To our boys. We love being your parents!

Compass Lost

"I don't think I should cram religion down my child's throat!"
Sound familiar? It was the theme of an entire generation.
Many of our era were raised by parents who found church boring while growing up, so they decided not to put their own kids through the same experience. "After all," went the rationale, "they can decide for themselves when they grow up."

Well, we are grown up. And rather than saying, "Thank you," many are asking, "How could you?"

Douglas Coupland's rather disturbing novel entitled *Life After God*, captures the spirit of a generation raised by parents who neglected spiritual instruction in the name of "protecting" their kids from dogmatism. It didn't work. The story is of a young man who travels from one empty experience to another in the vain hope of finding meaning in life—only to discover that he has no story beyond his own. The result? In his words . . .

> *I was wondering what was the logical end product of this recent business of my feeling less and less. Is feeling nothing the inevitable end result of believing in nothing? And then I got to feeling frightened—thinking that there might not actually be anything to believe in, in particular. I thought it would be such a sick joke to have to remain alive for decades and not believe in or feel anything.*[1]

He goes on to describe that his state of mind is in part the result of being "raised without religion by parents who had broken with their own pasts . . . who had raised their children clean of any ideology . . . at the end of history, or so they had wanted to believe."[2] In other words, his folks didn't want to cram religion down his throat. So he—like others of our generation—was given nothing in which to believe. The result? Freedom from the "shackles" of religious dogma caused imprisonment to a life without meaning.

Coupland's protagonist is confronting a harsh reality. Without God, nothing is sacred, so everything is meaningless. Or, in the words of King Solomon as he examined his life apart from God, "Meaningless! Meaningless! . . . Utterly meaningless! Everything is meaningless" (Ecclesiastes 1:2).

As parents, it is our job to give our children a framework for living—to equip them with a strong sense of identity that comes from knowing who made them, who they are, and how they fit within the grand drama of life. We must help them understand their own story from the Author's perspective, to enjoy the wonder that comes from knowing that with God, everything is sacred, so nothing is meaningless. Put simply, we want them to grow up with God.

When our son Shaun was about four years old, he walked a bit too far toward the deep end of a hotel swimming pool while I (Olivia) was momentarily distracted. He panicked as he began to swallow water. Thankfully, an older boy saw what was happening and quickly pulled him to safety. I noticed the scenario just as Shaun let out a cry of hysteria mixed with relief. Shaken by the thought of what could have happened, I committed to preventing it from ever happening again. I immediately enrolled him in swimming lessons.

For several months that summer, I drove Shaun fifteen miles each way three days per week to swim class. It was a hassle, for sure. But before long, he was able to tread water well enough to keep himself afloat. Mission accomplished.

Ours is an era in which nothing is considered sacred. To many, God is dead, distant, or perhaps worst of all, irrelevant. Objective truth—which should direct and explain life's experience, has been replaced by subjective opinion. Much like Shaun in the deep end of that pool, many have faced the panic of swallowing the water of a life without meaning. With Coupland, they are "frightened—thinking that there might not actually *be* anything to believe in, in particular."

We want something better for our kids. We refuse to shove them into the deep end of life without first teaching them how to swim. We want them to know that there *is* something to believe in, in particular.

A personal, loving God who created them for relationship.

A sense of purpose and meaning that transcends the often confusing and painful experiences they will endure.

Timeless truth which frames the choices they will face and explains the seemingly hapless circumstances of life.

A profound hope found only in Jesus Christ, which can overshadow the deepest despair.

May the bitter aftertaste of being raised without God inspire our generation to give the next something better. No, we don't want to "cram religion down the throats of our children." But we should let them in on the secret to the meaning of life that Solomon discovered: "Fear God and keep his commandments, for this is the whole duty of man" (Ecclesiastes 12:13).

The Compass

Consider the simplicity of a compass. It does one thing and one thing only. It points north. Not very impressive. That is, unless you are lost in the woods or are attempting to navigate the seas. When lost or disoriented, the fixed point of reference a compass provides may be the only source of clarity and direction available to help lead you home. Take away the compass, and you place the traveler at serious risk.

Sadly, for many in this generation, the spiritual compass of faith and character has been lost. We are ill-equipped for the journey, leaving us to wander through life with no clear sense of direction, no way to clarify what is right and what is wrong. Some have rejected the values of their parents. Others were raised in a family with no compass to pass. Either way, we are a generation that lacks the stability and confidence that come from knowing who we are, why we are here, and which way we are supposed to go.

It is that lost compass that we need to regain for our children. We seek to give them a framework for living—a Christian worldview—that includes the beliefs and values necessary to navigate the treacherous roads of life. They need a compass to continually establish "true north" in their lives, and it is our job as parents to give it to them, taking seriously the command of Deuteronomy 6:6-9.

These commandments that I give you today are to be upon your hearts. Impress them on your children. Talk about them when you sit at home and when you walk along the road, when you lie down and when you get up. Tie them as symbols on your hands and bind them on your foreheads. Write them on the doorframes of your houses and on your gates.

Once upon a time, parents considered this mandate a critical priority. When did that pattern change? When did Mom and Dad stop taking seriously their responsibility to equip the next generation with biblical beliefs and values?

In the Jewish tradition, faith was expressed first and foremost in the home, and secondarily in the synagogue. When Christianity emerged, the church and parents worked together in an intentional manner toward the same end. But as time passed, parents allowed the church to take the lead in the spiritual training of their children. Gradually, parents became passive observers of this all-important process, abdicating their role to the point that now, many Christians actually believe it is the job of the Sunday School to teach their children matters of faith. Certainly, the church is an important partner, but the primary responsibility still remains with Mom and Dad.

What is the greatest threat to successfully passing the compass to our children? In a word—negligence. Our days are filled with activity and responsibility. We live at such a fast pace that it is difficult even to *think* about the spiritual development of our children, let alone direct it. Most of us take our kids to church and hope that the forty-five minute lesson in Sunday School will get the job done. Deep within, however, we know it isn't enough. We feel the guilt. We regret the pace. We worry about the outcome. But we can't seem to break the cycle.

Every parent seeks to maximize the chances for each child to achieve success and happiness in life. That is the goal. But how do we do it? Where do we go for advice and guidance?

We start with advice from the only perfect parent—God Himself. The Bible contains both specific directives and broad guidelines with regard to the parenting process. God has revealed some things which can be known with certainty about our children and about giving a solid heritage to the next generation. It is upon these clear, biblical principles that we have attempted to build a model for equipping children to survive and thrive in a mixed-up world.

None of us can guarantee that our children will find success and happiness in life. But we can increase their odds. Toward that end, there are several things we as parents can do.

In part one, we will take a look at what the Scriptures say about our task. We will examine what we have called "Compass Principles," which govern and guide the process of giving a spiritual compass to the next generation. When we understand what the Scriptures tell us about our role as parents and about the nature and needs of our children, we will be better equipped to move forward.

In part two, we will examine what we call "Compass Beliefs," those core truths which provide a framework for living. When we teach our kids the basics of a Christian worldview, we give them a compass to help them recognize "true north" when confronted with deceptions and the challenges of living in a pluralistic society. Remember, as they grow they will be forced to navigate their way through life in a world where truth is subjective and reality changes depending upon individual opinion. In a day when what was once bizarre is considered commonplace, a solid grasp of what is "normal" from God's perspective will give our kids an incredible advantage in the game of life.

Compass beliefs are taken from the basic tenets of the Christian faith. Like a compass in the wilderness, they provide a fixed point of reference and explain the unseen realities of the spiritual life. They include the character of God, the existence of Satan, the authority of Scripture, the basic nature of man, our sin, and the gift of salvation through Jesus Christ.

In part three, we will learn how to equip our kids with several "Compass Values," which are necessary to find success and happiness in any generation. Like Solomon of old, we must say "listen my child" and share timeless wisdom on how to achieve excellence in the art of living.

Compass values are qualities that equip our children to counter their bent toward evil. Left to themselves, our kids will have no standard for normal, healthy living against which their attitudes and actions can be measured. Character values provide a framework of what is normal, to keep our children on track. The values include the worth and dignity of human life, personal responsibility, sexuality, integrity, respect, and hard work.

The list of compass beliefs and compass values presented in

parts two and three is by no means intended to be a comprehensive list. Rather, it is to serve as a launching point for the many beliefs and values that can be taught in such a manner. Each chapter explains the importance of and creative approaches to teaching one belief or value. As you read these chapters, a few disclaimers are in order.

First, we assume the reader to have embraced the Christian faith. We do not apologize for the position we represent in these chapters, but we recognize that some readers may not agree with what we consider an orthodox Christian view. We leave it to you the reader to discern those areas you find helpful or not, and welcome you to adapt some statements to your particular creed.

Second, we list several movies that can be helpful tools in the process of reinforcing certain beliefs and values. We do not recommend these films in their entirety, and strongly urge parents to view each film prior to using it with their children. Some contain offensive language and scenes through which parents should fast forward. Still, recognizing that most parents and children watch films together, we have tried to identify those which can be incorporated into the compass passing process.

Third, we encourage you to read every activity listed in the following chapters to spark your own creativity. We have provided target age ranges (in parenthesis) when appropriate, but most activities can be adapted to meet the specific ages of your children.

Compass passing is a lifelong process that happens in the everyday moments of life. Still, the old adage is true—those who fail to plan, plan to fail. Sadly, we rarely apply this principle to the parenting process. Let's break that cycle, shall we? May this book be an important step in your effort to intentionally pass to your children the spiritual compass they need and deserve.

PART 1

Compass Principles

→ *Chapter 1* ←

The Legacy Principle

⁓⁓⁓

here are several people in life you don't want to hear say "oops!" Your barber, your mechanic, and your surgeon are a few who come to mind. So do your parents. As parents, none of us want "oops" to sum up the influence we've had on the lives of our children. More often than we'd like, however, it will. That is, unless we learn to become intentional about what we give them during the few, short years they are in our care.

Scary, isn't it? Every time those tiny eyes stare up at you expectantly—seeking approval, needing comfort, or demanding peanut butter and jelly on white—your response could help determine whether or not that child becomes a happy, productive member of society or a bitter, messed-up "adult child of something or other." No pressure. It's all part of the process. You are somebody's mommy or daddy.

Like it or not, you are now the central focus of at least one little life—responsible for so much more than you bargained for back when you decided it was time to start a family. It kind of sneaks up on you, doesn't it? At first, it was sleepless nights and leaky diapers. Exhausting and disgusting, but a fair trade-off considering how cute the little bundle was. Then somebody raises the bar and you are faced with bumps and bruises, dinnertime spills, crayons on the wall, and the word "no!" in response to, well, everything. Still cute, but the trade-off is starting to seem a bit less fair. Before you know it, you are pole vaulting over issues you never imagined were part of the parenting package—like confronting that first cuss word, awkwardly trying to explain sex, or crying together after cruel teasing by the "in" crowd.

. . . . .

Home Decor

Taking Deuteronomy 6:6-9 literally— "write them on the door frames of your houses"— we intentionally decorate our home with pictures that have Bible verses printed on them. This reminds our children of God's words and of the Bible verses that are precious to our family.

G.A. Blue Jay, CA

. . . . .

We all face the future with that same unspoken concern over whether or not our kids will mature into happy, successful adults. We hope we are doing what's best for the little lives God has entrusted to our care. We, like you, had no practice round—no dress rehearsal. With the birth of our first son came the raising of the curtain, and we walked on stage for the performance of our lives. Like you, uncertainty and questions haunt our every move.

"Are we getting our lines right?"

"Have we missed any cues?"

"Do they like us?"

The outcome is still in question. Is it any wonder the role scares us to death?

Let's start with the bad news. There is no secret formula for becoming super parents—faster than a runny nose, more powerful than a temper tantrum, or able to leap willful rebellion in a single bound! Those "six easy steps to rearing perfect kids" we've all been searching for don't exist.

Now for the good news. With a little effort and a solid plan, you can give your kids what they need to build a framework for life. The key is to move from being passive to being proactive. Consider this book a friendly kick in the pants, a call to get your head in the game, an invitation to take the reins back from the school, church, television, and Nintendo!

Let's face it, there is nothing we care about more than our children. Yet, few of us ever move beyond accidental to intentional parenting. We stumble along, reacting to what happens rather than focusing our efforts toward a pre-defined goal. We may *hope* our kids will turn out well. But what are we *doing* to help them get there?

A Theology of Parenting

Theology. Just mentioning the word prompts an almost irresistible impulse to yawn. It conjures up images of old, bearded men crouched over thick, dusty books, contemplating deep but boring hypotheses. Using the word theology in the context of the parenting process seems out of place, even inappropriate. But it isn't. In fact, it is critically important that we understand what the Bible has to say about the role and responsibility of parents with regard to giving our children a spiritual compass.

Several passages of Scripture form the basis of what we call "a theology of parenting." Let's take a moment to examine a biblical perspective on what it means to be someone's mommy or daddy.

Generations

Someone has said that one of the best ways to assure yourself good health throughout life is to choose your parents very carefully. The genetic traits we inherit at conception play a major role in our physical well-being, and they are with us for life. So, to avoid getting stuck with a pool of crummy genes, make sure Mom and Dad come from healthy stock.

The truth is, we can't pick our parents. Nor can we alter the genetic blueprint we receive. There are certain traits and vulnerabilities that come as part of the package called life. What you are and what you will be physically is in large measure determined by the combined strengths and weaknesses of a long line of ancestors—for better or worse.

This same principle is true when it comes to our heritage. There are certain spiritual, emotional, and social patterns that are passed to us from our parents. And, just as the genetic code impacts our physical person for a lifetime, this heritage has a lifelong influence upon our attitudes, actions, and beliefs.

There is a sobering passage in the Book of Exodus that forms the basis of the first principle in our theology of parenting. While giving Moses the Ten Commandments on Mount Sinai, the Lord made this statement.

> *I, the Lord your God, am a jealous God, punishing the children for the sin of the fathers to the third and fourth generation of those who hate me, but showing love to a thousand generations of those who love me and keep my commandments (Exodus 20:5-6).*

On one hand, this statement bothers us. It seems harsh, even unfair. After all, we question, why should the innocent children and grandchildren suffer just because great-grandfather had a sin problem?

On the other hand, we can't deny the reality it reflects. God used an exaggerated statement to illustrate a very real principle in life. Think about it for a moment.

Going all the way back to Adam and Eve in the garden, there are certain hand-me-downs we all wear. We wear a sin nature, which gives us a propensity toward evil, toward self-destruction. Our sin nature is one of the human family hand-me-downs.

There are also certain specific family hand-me-down traits and characteristics we each receive from our ancestral lines. Those who were raised in the home of an alcoholic, for example, know all too well that their lives have been impacted by the sin of another. Statistics show that a high percentage of those who were abused as children end up abusing their own children. Why? It doesn't seem to make sense. But, as the Lord said on Mount Sinai, there are multi-generational impacts of sin. That is the bad news.

The good news is that there are also multi-generational impacts of righteousness. Remember what the Lord said, "But showing love to thousands who love me and keep my commandments." Those who live responsible, good lives tend to instill the same in their children. Just as bad tends to breed more bad, good tends to breed more good. It may not seem fair, but it is a reality we cannot deny.

· · · · ·

WWJD

We bought each of our boys WWJD bracelets as a reminder that no matter where they are, Jesus really does care how they handle the situation before them.

L.K. Clovis, CA

· · · · ·

This principle is the first we must understand as we develop a solid theology of parenting. It is what we call *The Legacy Principle*.

The Legacy Principle: What we do today will directly influence the multi-generational cycle of family traits, beliefs, and actions—for good or bad.

The Legacy Principle can work for us or it can work against us. Each of us has a choice whether or not to love God. That choice will affect our family.

Choices _____

Once upon a time, there was a man who had a son. Because he and his wife had been unable to conceive for a very long time, it was quite an event when the bundle of joy finally arrived. This man loved his boy more than life itself—and acted like it throughout the child's life. He would never have intentionally done anything to harm his boy or to prevent his success and happiness. But our first parenting principle came into play in the lives of Abraham and Isaac, and it had a multi-generational impact.

In the Book of Genesis, we read of an incident or two that demonstrate a pattern in Abraham's life that would have a profound influence upon future generations. We'll pick up the story just as Abraham (then called Abram) moved to Egypt.

> *Now there was a famine in the land, and Abram went down to Egypt to live there for a while because the famine was severe. As he was about to enter Egypt, he said to his wife Sarai, "I know what a beautiful woman you are. When the Egyptians see you, they will say, 'This is his wife.' Then they will kill me but will let you live. Say you are my sister, so that I will be treated well for your sake and my life will be spared because of you"* (Genesis 12:10-13).

As expected, the men took notice of Sarai's beauty. In fact, Pharaoh himself was told of this hot babe in the city, and he took her into his palace. Because they assumed Abram was her brother, he made out pretty well also. They gave Abram wealth and servants, and he was safe from harm. Yes sir, his little white lie was paying off. Until . . .

> *The Lord inflicted serious diseases on Pharaoh and his household because of Abram's wife Sarai. So Pharaoh summoned Abram. "What have you done to me?" he said. "Why didn't you tell me she was your wife? Why did you*

say, 'She is my sister,' so that I took her to be my wife? Now then, here is your wife. Take her and go!" Then Pharaoh gave orders about Abram to his men, and they sent him on his way, with his wife and everything he had" (Genesis 12:17-20).

Abram, this great man of faith, lied about Sarai, his lovely wife, in order to protect his own skin. Of course, we all mess up from time to time, don't we? Abram learned his lesson and moved on to avoid such stupid mistakes in the future, right? Well, not exactly. A few chapters later, shortly after God changed Abram's name to Abraham, we read of another incident.

Now Abraham moved on from there into the region of the Negev and lived between Kadesh and Shur. For a while he stayed in Gerar, and there Abraham said of his wife Sarah, "She is my sister." Then Abimelech king of Gerar sent for Sarah and took her.

But God came to Abimelech in a dream one night and said to him, "You are as good as dead because of the woman you have taken; she is a married woman."

Now Abimelech had not gone near her, so he said, "Lord, will you destroy an innocent nation? Did he not say to me, 'She is my sister,' and didn't she also say, 'He is my brother'? I have done this with a clear conscience and clean hands."

Then God said to him in the dream, "Yes, I know you did this with a clear conscience, and so I have kept you from sinning against me. That is why I did not let you touch her. Now return the man's wife, for he is a prophet, and he will pray for you and you will live. But if you do not return her, you may be sure that you and all yours will die" (Genesis 20:1-7).

Hard to believe, isn't it? Abraham made the exact same blunder again, placing yet another leader and nation at serious risk. He lied to protect himself, and nearly caused the death of many in the process. We read that Abimelech did do as the Lord commanded, and everything turned out all right in the end. But a pattern of deception in Abraham's life had developed, revealing a fundamental character flaw. He even recruited his wife to participate in the deception. Since the fallout of sinful choices extends to one's descendants, we would expect this skeleton in Abraham's closet to have a haunting influence beyond his own years.

As it turns out, the pattern of deception in Abraham's life was mirrored in the life of his beloved son Isaac and beyond. Let's take a look at an incident that occurred in the life of Isaac shortly after his father's death. Living in the land of Gerar (the same city his father had caused trouble in some time earlier) Isaac showed himself to be a chip off the old block.

So Isaac stayed in Gerar. When the men of that place asked him about his wife, he said, "She is my sister," because he was afraid to say, "She is my wife." He thought, "The men of this place might kill me on account of Rebekah, because she is beautiful" (Genesis 26:6-7).

This is like a bad movie. Isaac sinned against Rebekah in the same manner his father had sinned against Sarah years earlier. Adding insult to injury, it happened in the same city for the same pathetic reason—self-preservation! Fortunately, the Lord once again orchestrated events to prevent a tragedy.

When Isaac had been there a long time, Abimelech king of the Philistines looked down from a window and saw Isaac caressing his wife Rebekah. So Abimelech summoned Isaac and said, "She is really your wife! Why did you say, 'She is my sister'?"

Isaac answered him, "Because I thought I might lose my life on account of her."

Then Abimelech said, "What is this you have done to us?

One of the men might well have slept with your wife, and you would have brought guilt upon us" (Genesis 26:8-10).

Again, things turned out well in the end, but they did so in spite of Isaac's actions, not because of them. Though Rebekah and the nation of Gerar went unharmed due to Abimelech's fear of God, Isaac continued the pattern of deception started by his father. Sadly, the multi-generational cycle of lies blossomed and grew in the lives of his children and grandchildren.

Siblings

Isaac had two sons—Esau and Jacob. After Isaac's encounter with Abimelech, his wife and younger son partnered on a scheme that demonstrated the pattern of deception to be alive and well in the family.

Approaching the end of his life, Isaac decided it was time to formally transfer patriarchal responsibility to his older son, Esau. It was the custom of the time to lay hands on the oldest son as a symbol of special blessing and inheritance. This ceremony was of special significance to both generations because the one receiving this blessing was designated to be the head of the family from that day forward. Isaac instructed Esau to hunt and prepare a special meal to be enjoyed before bestowing the blessing. While Esau was on the hunt, Rebekah and Jacob discussed how they could subvert Isaac's

. . . . .

Date Night

When our oldest daughter turned thirteen, I took her on her first date. My reason was twofold: I wanted to turn a corner in our relationship and set the pace for a new father-daughter friendship. I also wanted to show her how a gentleman treats a lady. That evening is a precious memory for both of us, and to this day she still has the lacy paper coaster from the restaurant.

D.K. Columbus, OH

. . . . .

wishes and steal Esau's rightful blessing.

> *Rebekah said to her son Jacob, "Look, I overheard your father say to your brother Esau, 'Bring me some game and prepare me some tasty food to eat, so that I may give you my blessing in the presence of the Lord before I die.' Now, my son, listen carefully and do what I tell you: Go out to the flock and bring me two choice young goats, so I can prepare some tasty food for your father, just the way he likes it. Then take it to your father to eat, so that he may give you his blessing before he dies"* (Genesis 27:6-10).

They prepared the meal, disguised Jacob to look, smell, and feel like his more masculine brother, and proceeded to trick Isaac. Take special notice of how smooth, clever, and irreverent Jacob became when the moment of deception arrived.

> *He went to his father and said, "My father."*
> *"Yes, my son," he answered. "Who is it?"*
> *Jacob said to his father, "I am Esau your firstborn. I have done as you told me. Please sit up and eat some of my game so that you may give me your blessing."*
> *Isaac asked his son, "How did you find it so quickly, my son?"*
> *"The Lord your God gave me success," he replied.*
> *Then Isaac said to Jacob, "Come near so I can touch you, my son, to know whether you really are my son Esau or not"* (Genesis 27:18-21).

Isaac felt Jacob's hands, which Rebekah had disguised using animal hair. Since he felt like Esau, but sounded like Jacob, Isaac became confused. To assure himself, he asked Jacob again.

"Are you really my son Esau?"

"I am," he replied.

This was no "little white" lie. Jacob looked his father straight in the eyes and intentionally deceived the old, dying man. Like his father and grandfather before him, Jacob chose a lie in order to avoid the potential consequences of the truth. The pattern continued, creating a rift in the relationship with his brother so severe that Jacob had to flee his home and live in a distant land to avoid the wrath of Esau.

The cycle didn't end with Jacob. You know the story. Jealous of their younger brother, ten of Jacob's sons sold their sibling into slavery, then lied about it to their father, saying that Joseph was eaten by a wild animal. Once again, the pattern of deception emerged. Just as the law stated, the poison of Abraham's sin reached across four generations, destroying reputations, risking lives, and tearing relationships apart.

God was able to carry out His majestic plan despite the deception of these patriarchs. One can't help wondering, however, how things might have been different for this family had the pattern been one of honesty rather than lies.

The story of Abraham and his descendants serves as an important lesson for parents in every age. Abraham never intended to hurt his son or his grandchildren. Still, that which seemed like a minor character flaw had a profound impact upon several generations. Of course, Isaac, Jacob, and the others each made their own choices in life. They were not victims. They could not rightfully blame Abraham for their own sinful actions. But they were heavily influenced by the negative cycle he began.

Passing the Positive

What is true about passing negative cycles is equally true of positive cycles. In fact, one of the central themes of the Bible is the hope of new beginnings. We are all heavily influenced by multi-generational patterns, but none of us are victims to them. It is possible to break away from the bad and launch a new era of good for ourselves and future generations.

As we've already seen, the sin of Abraham impacted his son, his grandson, and his great-grandchildren. But not all of them. Jacob's ten oldest sons adopted the ways of granddad. But Joseph, his eleventh, did not. Obviously, the sin of his ten older brothers had a dramatic impact upon his life. But Joseph managed to break the cycle. He lived an obedient life, refusing to let go of the Lord's hand, though he had every reason to do so. He did not lie, even when doing so would have saved his neck. In short, Joseph broke the cycle of betrayal and deception. The result? An entire generation was saved from certain death, and his own family was preserved for many generations.

After being sold into slavery by his brothers, Joseph helped his master achieve great success. He became like a son to Potiphar. But Joseph became the victim of another lie told by his master's wife and was thrown into prison. Again, he gained favor in the eyes of the prison warden and was promoted to a respected position (at least by prison life standards). Eventually, due to his faithfulness and integrity, Joseph was given an audience before Pharaoh himself. By interpreting Pharaoh's dream, Joseph was instrumental in saving the known world from famine. In the end, he was promoted to prime minister—second in command to Pharaoh alone.

What made the difference in Joseph's life? Why, against all odds, was he able to make the Legacy Principle work for him rather than against him? We are given a clue in a scene described in the Book of Genesis. Shortly after Jacob's death, the ten brothers came before Joseph seeking pardon from the retribution they deserved. Here is what happened.

When Joseph's brothers saw that their father was dead, they said, "What if Joseph holds a grudge against us and pays us back for all the wrongs we did to him?" So they sent word to Joseph, saying, "Your father left these instructions before he died: 'This is what you are to say to Joseph: I ask you to forgive your brothers

the sins and the wrongs they committed in treating you so
badly.' Now please forgive the sins of the servants of the God of
your father." When their message came to him, Joseph wept.
   His brothers then came and threw themselves down before
him. "We are your slaves," they said (Genesis 50:15-18).

Make note of the fact that the brothers have not yet broken
the pattern of deception. Even now they lie, saying the request
is from Jacob rather than themselves. It is at this point in the
story that Joseph makes a profound statement which tells us
why he was different.

But Joseph said to them, "Don't be afraid. Am I in the place of
God? You intended to harm me, but God intended it for good
to accomplish what is now being done, the saving of many
lives. So then, don't be afraid. I will provide for you and your
children." And he reassured them and spoke kindly to them
(Genesis 50:19-21).

You see, Joseph refused to be held in bondage to the past. He
would not be a victim to the patterns that had enslaved several
generations. Recognizing that God is in control of the good and
the bad, he chose to forgive his brothers and let go of the bag-
gage of his past. Realizing that his choices would impact many,
he intentionally created a new era for his family. In the end, even
those who had wronged him benefited from his choice. Joseph
provided for them and their children.

There are numerous examples in the Bible of men and
women like Joseph. They refused to remain in bondage to the
negative cycles of the past, choosing to create positive cycles for
future generations. A quick read through the Books of Kings and
Chronicles will reveal men who chose not to follow in the foot-
steps of their wayward fathers. Instead, they did what was right
in the sight of the Lord. Many of the kings did continue in their
fathers' sins, perpetuating the generational bias toward evil. In

the midst of it all, however, a descendant would surface who chose to break the cycle. After a string of rulers who made wrong choices, it is an oasis to read, as in 2 Kings 12, "Joash did what was right in the eyes of the Lord." He was one who broke the cycle. We can too!

The Legacy Principle worked against Abraham. He passed his negative traits to future generations, failing to recognize and intentionally counter them. The question we must ask is whether we are doing the same, and if so, how we—like Joseph, Joash, and others—can break the cycle. Once again, the Legacy Principle tells us that what we do today will directly influence the multi-generational cycle of family traits, beliefs, and actions—for good or bad.

Giving What We're Living _____

It is clear from the examples we've seen that we tend to give what we live. Abraham's life of lies was passed to his children and grandchildren. We can't help but wonder how different things would have been had Abraham modeled truth instead. The negative patterns that started with his sin could have been avoided if he had been obedient. So it is in our lives. We can't pass a positive spiritual legacy to future generations if we don't have a right relationship with God ourselves. We can't give what we don't live.

Some parents have the mistaken impression that they can focus on the spiritual training of their children

> .....
> ### Reach Out
>
> We support a child through Compassion International and talk about how important all people are to God. We use the picture of the child as an example that color and race do not matter to God. It is also an example of our duty to be generous with what God has given us.
>
> *D.H. Colorado Springs, CO*
> .....

without seriously confronting their own spiritual condition. The message given to their children is "do what I say, not what I do!" It doesn't work. The first and most important step in this process is making sure we have our own hearts right with God. Right relationship with God starts with the realization that we are all sinful and need His forgiveness. It requires a conscious decision to trust in the sacrifice of His Son Jesus Christ, and to submit our will to His. As the Scriptures tell us . . .

> *For all have sinned and fall short of the glory of God, and are justified freely by his grace through the redemption that came by Christ Jesus* (Romans 3:23-24).

> *For the wages of sin is death, but the gift of God is eternal life in Christ Jesus our Lord* (Romans 6:23).

> *For God so loved the world that he gave his one and only Son, that whoever believes in him shall not perish but have eternal life. For God did not send his Son into the world to condemn the world, but to save the world through him. Whoever believes in him is not condemned, but whoever does not believe stands condemned already because he has not believed in the name of God's one and only Son* (John 3:16-18).

Passing a spiritual compass requires that we first possess one. Once we have established a right relationship with God, we are ready to begin making the Legacy Principle work for us and our children, rather than against us.

Bottom Line

God has given both a mandate and a model to parents for teaching children values. The Scriptures declare and describe a principle— or law—which provides the primary motivation for passing a spiritual compass to our children. According to the Legacy Principle, what we do today will directly influence the multi-generational cycle of family traits, beliefs, and actions—for good or bad.

Chapter 2

The Likelihood Principle

*P*aul walks inside the local filling station to pay for ten gallons of gasoline he has pumped into the broken-down bucket-of-bolts he calls a car. The bumper sticker on the back reads, "My other car is a Mercedes." Of course, it isn't. But Paul prefers laughing at his situation to crying over it. Unfulfilled in his job, eager to get ahead, and tired of existing at the lower end of middle class, Paul is hoping this will be his lucky day. He can feel it in his bones, that sense of anticipation as he points to the daily lottery ticket display. "I'll take five please."

Paul hurries back to the car and pulls out a penny. He looks forward to this bit of excitement each day after his long, mundane shift at work.

Scratch. Nothing.
Scratch. Nothing.
Scratch. Nothing.
Scratch. A free ticket!
Scratch. Nothing.

Unsatisfied, Paul pulls away from the gasoline pump and stops in front of the window. "I've won a free ticket. Can I have it please?" The attendant hands him his last hope for the day. Scratch. Nothing.

Once again, Paul tried to beat the odds. Once again, he returns home five dollars poorer. "Oh, well," he muses. "Maybe tomorrow."

Unfortunately, millions of us throw away hard-earned money every day in the vain hope that we will finally beat the odds. In an effort to get rich quick, we seek to defy common sense. Knowing full well that we have one chance in millions, we still play.

Life is a game of risk. There are always odds to play. Sometimes, like Paul, we take a chance on a sure loss. And, like Paul, we lose. But it doesn't have to be that way. It is possible to play odds that are in our favor.

If we want wealth, for example, there are better ways to acquire it than the lottery. It may take more time and commitment, but our "odds" improve dramatically when we play the "stay out of debt, save, and invest" game. Certainly, there is no guarantee we will get there. But our chances are better than one in millions.

Show us a person who selects stable investments that tend to grow, and we'll show you a person who accumulates long-term wealth. Show us a person, on the other hand, who chases every multi-level marketing scheme, and we'll show you a person who suffers the consequences of short-term loss after short-term loss.

If we want to remain healthy, our chances improve when we eat properly and exercise regularly. Of course, we can still become ill. But those who treat their bodies right tend to feel better and live longer. So say the odds.

What is true of so many areas of life is also true of parenting. We can choose to play with or against the odds. But what are those odds, and how do we make them work for us rather than against us? This question leads us into a second vital principle in our theology of parenting.

Train Up a Child _____

In his ancient book of sage wisdom, Proverbs, King Solomon penned what are perhaps the most frequently quoted words in all of Scripture with regard to the child rearing process. He said, "Train a child in the way he should go, and when he is old he will not turn from it" (Proverbs 22:6). This passage is describing a principle we can embrace as we develop our theology of parenting. It is what we have labeled the Likelihood Principle.

The Likelihood Principle: In the context of healthy relationships, children tend to embrace the values of their parents.

The good news for us parents is that the odds are strongly in our favor! When cultivated properly, the natural tendency is for children to adopt the values we model and reinforce in their lives.

. . . . .

Family Gift

We always read the Christmas story from Luke 2 before we have our family candlelight dinner on Christmas Eve. Last year our oldest daughter memorized Luke 2 and recited it as a gift to the family before we ate.

T.B. Colorado Springs, CO

. . . . .

Several years ago, I (Kurt) attended a debate between two theologians. On one side was a liberal theologian and writer who saw God as a mystical, ever-changing force rather than a perfect, never-changing person. On the other side was a leading Christian apologist who was defending the orthodox view of God. Knowing the reputation of this particular apologist, I expected him to destroy the arguments of the liberal theologian—demonstrating the intellectual superiority of orthodox Christianity. I was not disappointed. The arguments were strong. The debate was dominated by the orthodox view. The truth prevailed once again!

The following day, I spoke to a coworker who had also attended the debate. "Wasn't it great? Our guy won the debate hands-down! He showed just how silly the liberal view is."

After a long pause, my coworker made an interesting comment.

"Yes, our guy presented the stronger case. But something troubles me."

"What?" I asked.

"Even though I had to agree with the orthodox view, I wanted to agree with the other gentleman."

I was confused. "What do you mean?"

"Our guy seemed arrogant, rude, and harsh in his demeanor. The other guy was very gentle, gracious, and kind. So, while the orthodox arguments may have been stronger, it is possible that many in the audience rejected them because they were turned off by the person presenting them. Our guy may have won the intellectual debate, but the other guy won the battle for the hearts of the audience. Which, I wonder, is more effective?"

That experience illustrated an important point. We are often drawn to accept the views of those we like and reject the views of those we dislike, regardless of who makes the strongest case. The key to convincing others to accept our values goes beyond articulating a strong argument. It requires building a solid relationship.

If the Likelihood Principle is going to work for us as parents, we must focus on relationship. It is easy to accept and embrace the beliefs of those we love and admire. It is quite difficult to accept and embrace the values of those we dislike or scarcely know. Thus, teaching values in the context of a loving, affirming relationship is highly effective. But to do so in the context of a distant or antagonistic relationship can do more harm than good. Consider Kathleen's story.

Kathleen grew up in a Christian home. She attended church regularly with Mom, Dad, and her siblings. The family Bible was prominently displayed on the coffee table in the den. There was prayer before every meal—even in restaurants. From all appearances, you would describe Kathleen as living in the ideal Christian family. And in many ways, you would be right. But there was one problem: Kathleen and her father didn't get along.

During childhood, Kathleen barely got to know her dad. As a successful professional, he was kept away from home during the week by long hours and business travel. As an adult Sunday School teacher, his weekends were consumed by study and church activities. His heart was right, but his schedule was full. Therefore, little relationship was fostered during Kathleen's critical childhood years.

During adolescence, Kathleen struggled with low self-worth. But since no foundation of trust had been built between them, she never shared these feelings with her father. Between acne, roller-coaster emotions, and boys, Kathleen could have used a daddy's hug. And he would have given it had she invited him into her world. But she didn't.

By the time Kathleen was a junior in high school, the tension between her and her father was thick. Whenever he led the family in prayer or tried to read a short devotion, her body stiffened. As the family marched dutifully into the church behind her father, the deacon, Kathleen felt sick to her stomach. In those moments, every fault in his life was magnified, and profound disrespect burned her heart. *What a hypocrite!* Kathleen thought behind her wooden stare. *If "Mr. Holier-Than-Thou" thinks he can cram this religious garbage down my throat, he's got another think coming.*

When Kathleen left home as a young adult, she left the faith of her family as well. Despite her father's best intentions and diligent efforts to instill Christian values, they didn't take. She rejected the values, not because they were bad, but because they were his. You see, Kathleen needed more than mere knowledge of her father's faith. She needed a relationship with her father's heart. Without the latter, she wasn't interested in the former.

There are countless Kathleens in the world. Raised in a Christian home, they were given a solid spiritual legacy, but they rejected the values they were taught. Why? People reject the faith for many reasons. Quite often, it is because the relationship with Mom, Dad, or both was weak. Don't misunderstand. Kathleen is responsible for her own decision to reject the faith. Her father is not to blame for the choices she made. But one can't help wondering how things might have been different if he had been as intentional about spending time playing with and getting to know Kathleen as he was about praying over meals and getting the family to church on time.

The old adage is true: People don't care how much you know until they know how much you care. Our children need more than a list of precepts and principles to embrace. If we want the values we teach them to stick, we must apply heavy amounts of the glue called love. You cannot have one without the other. Children perceive parental instruction through emotional lenses. Those lenses are framed by the quality of the parent-child relationship. Yes, the odds are in our favor, and kids tend to adopt the values of their parents. But outside the context of strong relationship, the odds are not nearly as good as we might hope.

No Guarantees

Many have understood Proverbs 22:6 to be a promise, a guarantee, a deal with the Almighty. The rules are simple. If Mom and Dad hold up their end of the bargain—taking the kids to church and living a decent life at home—God will uphold His end of the bargain—making sure the kids ultimately turn out well. Sounds good, but it is not that simple.

While Proverbs 22:6 is indeed a verse of hope, it is not a promise. Not all biblical passages are promises to claim. Many, like this one, are principles to heed. You see, the Proverbs are divinely inspired statements describing the patterns and principles which govern the universe, including human behavior. In an effort to clarify confusion over this particular verse, a panel of respected, conservative theologians from Dallas Seminary explained it like this. . . .

> Some parents . . . have sought to follow this directive but without this result. Their children have strayed from the godly training the parents gave them. This illustrates the nature of a "proverb." A proverb is a literary device whereby a general truth is brought to bear on a specific situation. Many of the proverbs are not absolute guarantees for they express truths that are necessarily conditioned by prevailing circumstances. . . . Though the proverbs are generally and usually true, occasional exceptions may be noted. This may be because of self-will or deliberate disobedience of an individual who chooses to go his own way—the way of folly instead of the way of wisdom. For that he is held responsible. It is generally true, however, that most children who are brought up in Christian homes, under the influence of godly parents who teach and live God's standards, follow that training.[1]

During my (Kurt) years as Director of Correspondence for Focus on the Family, I led a team of caring people who responded to hundreds of letters from hurting parents. Rather than reaping the anticipated rewards of the parenting process, they were suffering the pain and guilt associated with teen and adult children who had rejected their faith. Despite their best efforts to model and teach Christian values, and to foster a strong relationship, the kids went a different way. The collective voice of these parents serves as a sobering reminder that there are no guarantees. You could sense the pain, confusion, and anger as they penned a common theme.

"I claimed Proverbs 22:6—training him up in the way he should go. Now he is old, and he *has* departed from it! What did I do wrong? What can I do now?"

The same verse, which was a source of motivation and hope in the early years of parenting, has turned into a source of overwhelming guilt and confusion in the later years. After playing the odds, they feel they lost the game.

More often than not, parents with a wayward child place themselves under the heavy burden of self-condemnation. But when we blame ourselves, it is not only destructive, but it is also wrong. Every person on earth has been given a free will—the ability to accept or reject truth. If we have done our best as parents, mistakes and all, we have fulfilled our responsibility. Now the child must fulfill his.

We have every right to feel heartache, to reel from the pain of rejection. It is natural to experience confusion, hurt, even anger. We have the right to cry. But we do not have the right to blame ourselves. Even if a parent tried to do so, he or she could not make a child reject Christian faith and values. That is a choice each individual makes for him or herself.

> .....
> ## *Pray for Others*
> We offer up prayers for our sons when they are sick. Now, when one of their friends is sick or they've heard about someone who is hurt, they pray for that person, and our sons remind us to pray for them too.
> *S.K. Clovis, CA*
> .....

Many parents have learned the hard way a lesson we must all face: In the game of parenting, there are no guarantees. No parent, regardless of how hard he or she tries, is assured that his or her children will embrace the beliefs and values he or she tries to instill. Just ask God, the only perfect parent in history.

God knows the pain of rejection. His children have resisted His paternal care and guidance from the beginning of time. Genesis chapter three describes the beginning of a long line of rejection: Adam and Eve chose to go their own way rather than to obey the Father. Despite God's perfect parenting, free will was and is part of the mix, as Jesus illustrated through His Story of the Prodigal Son, told in the fifteenth chapter of the Book of Luke.

In this well-known story, the father, representing God, did not try to prevent the son from making a foolish choice. He granted him the freedom to decide his own course in life, even when that meant squandering away his entire future. As a result, he experienced the pain of rejection—and the joy of eventual reconciliation.

If God Himself accepts the possibility of rejection, so must we. None of us are perfect parents. All of us are called to do our best. The odds are in our favor if we do. But there are no guarantees.

Secret Formula

Have you ever known one of those couples who has been blessed with terrific kids? You know the ones. They are the family you watch from afar, wondering how in the world they got so lucky, or did so well. It is almost as if they have discovered a secret formula for raising great kids.

We have been fortunate over the years to build relationships with some of those couples, watching over the long haul as they navigate the varied and perilous stages of parenthood. Their children have grown from little kids to young adults, and though imperfect, have turned out quite well. Many of them are approaching the end of the parenting journey, and are reaping the rewards of having done some things right. Let us give you a peek into what we've learned from these little known, greatly respected examples of parental success.

The Piersmas, a family of seven, had a major influence on my (Olivia) life as a teenager and young adult. Having come from a broken, troubled home, I had no model of what a healthy family could be. I befriended Darcee Piersma during junior high, and we remain best friends more than twenty years later. I spent as much time as possible at Darcee's house, partly to escape the conflict in my own home, and partly because I was in awe of what I observed there. Unlike my own home, Dad, Mom, and the kids actually seemed to enjoy one another. They loved unconditionally. They talked over the evening dinner table, and seemed to care about what the others were saying. They laughed together, played together, teased together, even took vacations together. Through the good and bad, they liked being together. Their enjoyment was almost contagious.

Decades later, the Piersmas still enjoy one another. They've been separated by distance as the kids have left home to start families of their own. The children have gone through struggles. Still, the close ties established early remain strong. The kids have embraced Dad and Mom's faith, even during an era in which Dad and Mom wavered themselves. We can't help but wonder, when so many families struggle just to survive, what "secret formula" helped the Piersma family thrive?

After watching the Ledbetter family in action for nearly twenty years, we have come to admire and covet the success they've experienced in the parenting process. With two grown children and a teenager at home, Otis and Gail Ledbetter are beginning to reap the rewards of having done something right. All three kids consider Mom and Dad to be among their best friends. All three kids have adopted Mom and Dad's values. Certainly, they have their own opinions and preferences, but the apple has remained pretty close to the tree. Why, when so many kids are rejecting the faith and values of their parents, did the Ledbetter children readily embrace theirs? What is their "secret formula"?

If you ask Mike and Terri Beidermann to tell you about their four teenagers, be prepared for an extensive bragging session. They are proud of their kids, as they should be. Though by no means perfect, the Beidermann children reflect the love and investment of diligent, intentional parents. They have good morals, manners, discipline, and a healthy dose of success. They also have questions, struggles, failures, and a healthy dose of opposition to what their parents believe. But they continue to believe. They embrace the faith and values modeled by Mom and Dad even when it is unpopular to do so. Once again, the "secret formula" has worked wonders.

What is this "secret formula" for successfully passing our values to the next generation? What is the common thread between these and other homes that seem to have beaten the odds in the parenting process? As we've watched over the years, we have seen the same important ingredient. The specific tone and makeup of each family varies, but the "secret formula" is the same. Every one of these couples discovered and mastered the art of enjoying their children, and allowing their children to enjoy them. Put simply, they had fun together!

Observing the Piersmas, the Ledbetters, the Beidermanns, and other families has convinced us that laugher and fun are incredibly powerful tools in the process of passing values. While

> .....
> ## Reminders
> My daughter reminds us when we fret over something that needs repairs or when we spend too much time working around the house. "People are more important than things."
> D.H. Colorado Springs, CO
> .....

much of this book is dedicated to giving principles and ideas on how to teach our kids, it assumes a context of enjoying our kids. That, we believe, is one of the most important ingredients for increasing the odds.

When I (Kurt) spend time wrestling with our boys in the basement, I have done more to make our values stick than when I read them a Bible passage. Both are important, but the former makes the latter more meaningful.

When I (Olivia) play a round of "Go Fish" with six-year-old Shaun, he learns to enjoy me as a person, not merely obey me as a parent. Again, both are important, but the former makes the latter easier to swallow.

Everyone has the right to speak. We must earn the right to be listened to. As parents, we must realize that when we play with our kids today we are earning the right to shape their values tomorrow. Remember that they are more likely to embrace the values of someone they love and enjoy than someone they don't. So let's adopt the secret formula that seems to have worked so well for so many parents. Let's have fun with our kids!

The Heritage Builders book *Family Fragrance* is an excellent resource to help you get those good times rolling. It includes ideas on how to have fun and how to build a foundation for strong relationships. It is filled with creative suggestions on how to foster an aroma of love in your family, establishing the best possible environment for teaching values and making them stick.

Report Card

Bruce is the father of two. He has been spending time each week conducting activities designed to teach the faith to his children. He has also been busy at work and various other commitments. Concerned that he might not be spending enough time with his kids, he decided to take a risk. Bruce sat the kids down one evening and asked them to grade the job he was doing as a dad.

"Tonight, I want you to fill out a 'Report Card for Dad' to grade me on how I am doing," Bruce explained. "There are several things the Lord expects me to do as your father, and I want your opinion on how well I am doing."

The kids were surprised, but more than willing to go along. So they spent the next few minutes grading Dad by completing the report card he had developed.

REPORT CARD FOR DAD

Prepared by Brooks and Brianna

Description	Grade
1. Dad shows that he loves me	_____
2. Dad is interested in my feelings	_____
3. Dad spends enough time with me	_____
4. Dad listens to what I say	_____
5. Dad trusts me	_____
6. Dad enjoys being with me	_____
7. Dad is truthful	_____
8. Dad makes the family a priority in his life	_____
9. Dad is fair in his decisions	_____
10. Dad gives me the right number of chores	_____
11. Dad disciplines me when I deserve it	_____
12. Dad admits when he is wrong	_____
13. Dad controls his anger and words	_____
Overall Grade for My Dad	_____

On a scale of 1-10, with 10 being the best, what kind of relationship do you want to have with your dad?

Considering all things, on the same scale, where are you today in your relationship with your dad?

If you could have your dad start today to do 1–3 things for you, what would they be?

Once completed, Bruce had an opportunity to discuss his grades with the kids. As expected, he received a different rating depending upon the child. Brianna, for example, graded him down on fair discipline but high on showing love. Brooks, on the other hand, thought the discipline was okay, but felt that Dad didn't spend enough time with him. As promised, Bruce resisted the urge to defend himself. The goal was to discover how the kids perceived his efforts, regardless of what Bruce thought of his efforts. Bruce shared later that the exercise, though painful, was extremely helpful as he assessed his relationship with his kids. It created an opportunity to clarify expectations, and to discover areas in which he might improve as a father. The risk was more than worth it.

Bruce understands the power of the Likelihood Principle. He realizes that it is not enough to merely instruct his children. He must also maintain and foster a strong relationship with them in order to create a context for success.

Bottom Line

The Likelihood Principle says that, in the context of healthy relationships, children tend to embrace the values of their parents. While Proverbs 22:6 is not a promise or a guarantee, it teaches us that the odds for successfully passing Christian values increase dramatically when we cultivate a fun, loving relationship with our children.

→ *Chapter 3* ←

The Lenses Principle

*N*early every suburban neighborhood has that one dog that strikes terror in the heart of every little kid. My block was no exception. I (Kurt) was one of the kids, and Rasha was the dog. My buddies and I were ordinary five-year-old boys, but Rasha was no ordinary dog. Rasha was a Great Dane who looked more like a small horse than a large dog. All the neighborhood kids were convinced that he could leap over the fence whenever he pleased. Needless to say, we avoided going near his fence and lived in fearful anticipation that sooner or later, Rasha would get loose from his yard and seek out young, tender children as an afternoon snack.

Finally, to everyone's terror, the day arrived. One of the neighborhood kids screamed out for all to hear, "Rasha's loose! Run for your lives!" No quicker were the words out of his mouth than every kid on the block scattered to the nearest available house. In less than five seconds, a street full of children at play became empty, lifeless pavement. It was a matter of hours before the first brave soul dared to set foot outside, only to discover that it had been a false alarm. Rasha had been napping the whole time!

What we believe to be true has a direct impact upon our behavior, whether or not that belief is consistent with reality. Rasha posed no actual threat to any of us, but our panic was genuine nonetheless. Had we investigated the accuracy of the warning before acting upon it, our reaction would have been quite different. By accepting as fact that which was actually a lie, we chose the wrong course of action.

Such is the pattern of life. We live consistent with what we believe to be true, even when we are mistaken. The more our understanding of the world conforms to reality, the better our choices will be. The more we operate under false assumptions, the worse our judgment becomes.

Life Map

Few things are as frustrating as the effort to locate a new address using a less than precise map. I (Olivia) am one of those people who tends to trust my memory when listening to directions, usually missing certain details. In contrast, Kurt typically asks probing questions about distances between streets and landmarks, using crayons and a metric ruler to draw a map that will be color-coded and to scale. The directions in hand when we pull out of our driveway generally end up somewhere in between these two extremes.

We have entered many social gatherings late and tense as a result of my part of our combined mapping efforts. We either miss the right street, turn onto the wrong street, head the wrong direction on the right street, or head the right direction on the wrong street! Once we have found the general area, we circle the block several times before stopping at a pay phone to call. It can be so embarrassing!

Just as a reliable map is essential for reaching an unfamiliar location, so must our understanding of the world be accurate if we hope to reach our objectives in life. Imagine the frustration and futility of trying to find a specific location in Denver using a map of Dallas. Yet, we can easily cause our children to try to navigate life based upon a faulty worldview, and the consequences can be far worse than embarrassing.

.....

The Club

When my younger daughter was in the fifth grade some of the students formed "the club." It was quite an elite group, and the other children's worth was valued as to whether they were in "the club" or not. My daughter didn't seem affected by my reminder that they were being unkind and snobbish with their "club." God has His ways, however. One day my daughter came home devastated that she had been kicked out of "the club." At that point, God helped her to see how she had been treating others wrongfully.

M.H. Littleton, CO

.....

If life is generally difficult, but your map says it should be generally easy, you will encounter disillusionment. Our beliefs about life will not change its reality one bit. They will, however, cause us to develop expectations and make decisions that are inconsistent with what is true. We will be making wrong turns on a regular basis.

Those who follow the wrong map may become frustrated over the inefficiency of their efforts. Other people seem to make much more progress than they do, reaching their goals with far less exertion. They fail to understand that advancing toward a given objective is not dependent upon the amount of energy expended, but upon whether or not one is heading in the right direction.

A critical part of our role as parents is helping our children develop a life map that is consistent with reality. We must replace false directions with an accurate map.

It may seem elementary to suggest that we must help our

kids understand and accept truth. But there are several factors that add complexity to what should be a simple process. Distinguishing the truth from lies can be difficult, especially when lies are perceived as the truth.

As parents, we must not forget that we are in enemy occupied territory. There is a great deceiver who has mastered the process of manipulating the drama of life to blind our eyes to the truth and to confuse our perception of reality. Jesus pulled no punches when He described the unpleasant but undeniable reality of Satan's primary weapon.

When he lies, he speaks his native language, for he is a liar and the father of lies (John 8:44).

If we are abused, we know it. When we are tempted or oppressed, we know it. But if we are deceived, we don't know it! That is why lies are such powerful weapons in the battle for the hearts and minds of our children. Satan understands the power and influence of deception. Do we?

Fortunately, we have an even more powerful weapon in this battle—truth. We can dispel the darkness of lies with the light of truth. Jesus makes it quite clear in an earlier passage.

If you hold to my teaching, you are really my disciples. Then you will know the truth, and the truth will set you free (John 8:31-32).

Tragically, our tendency as fallen people is to reject what is true in favor of what is comfortable, and to choose what is familiar over what is right. As painful as a lie may be, Jesus knew that it is often preferred over reality.

This is the verdict: Light has come into the world, but men loved darkness instead of light because their deeds were evil (John 3:19).

In his classic work *Mere Christianity,* C.S. Lewis shed light upon what happens when we seek what is comfortable rather than what is true. ". . . comfort is the one thing you cannot get by looking for it. If you look for truth, you may find comfort in the end: If you look for comfort you will not get either comfort or truth—only soft soap and wishful thinking to begin with and, in the end, despair."[1]

In the battle for the hearts and minds of our children, we must recognize that they need our intentional guidance to counter the deceptions of life. Otherwise, they will accept an imperfect life map, altering their view of reality. Any points of deviation from the truth must be identified and corrected with the truth as soon as possible.

So how does this apply to our theology of parenting? By understanding that children enter this world with blurred vision—with an inability to recognize reality—we can become intentional about helping them sort through deception and recognize truth. It is what we call the Lenses Principle.

The Lenses Principle: Our children need the corrective lenses of truth in order to navigate the deceptive roads of life.

We live in a culture that has in large part rejected this principle, with tragic consequences. One of the reasons those beliefs and behaviors once considered depraved are now considered normal is that parents are reluctant to teach their children a standard of absolute moral truth.

In his number one best-selling book, *The Closing of the American Mind,* Allan Bloom provided commentary on the generally accepted premise of our culture.

There is one thing a professor can be absolutely certain of: almost every student entering the university believes, or says he believes, that truth is relative. If this belief is put to the

test, one can count on the students' reaction: they will be
uncomprehending. That anyone should regard the proposition
as non self-evident astonishes them, as though he were calling
into question 2 + 2 = 4. . . . The danger they have been taught
to fear from absolutism is not error but intolerance. . . .
Openness—and the relativism that makes it the only plausible
stance in the face of various claims to truth and various ways
of life and kinds of human beings—is the great insight of our
times. The true believer is the real danger. . . . The point is
not to correct the mistakes and really be right; rather it is not
to think you are right at all.[2]

Dialogue and debate over what is true have diminished due
to the commonly held view that all truth is relative. Each person
decides for himself what is true. Rather than looking up for
understanding, this perspective compels us to look within. We
are encouraged to become our own source of truth, and our own
god. Thus, parents who force specific moral absolutes down the
throats of their children are not only naïve, but also dangerous!

Some time ago the Associated Press released a story about E.
Frenkel, one of the then Soviet Union's increasing number of
psychics. He planned to use his extraordinary abilities to stop
a freight train after claiming to successfully stop bicycles, auto-
mobiles, and streetcars. E. Frenkel stepped onto the track facing
the oncoming train, confident that his psychic-biological powers
would stop it. It didn't work, and he was killed instantly. In the
reality created by E. Frenkel, the train stopped. In the reality
created by God, it didn't.

No matter how strongly we believe that our view of truth is
right for us, if it is inconsistent with reality, it isn't right! The law
of gravity is just as tough on the guy who thinks he can fly as it
is on the rest of us. Individual belief does not alter absolute truth.
Our culture's progression toward relativism is nothing more than
a rejection of the light in favor of darkness. Our children must

discover truth for themselves. But that does not mean that we should allow them to create their own truth. Absolute truth is real, and it has been revealed in the Bible. Our role as parents is to guide our children in their discovery of biblical truth.

Losing "Normal"

It is a proven fact that time slows dramatically the minute Mom or Dad declares "bedtime!" to the children. Although intended to get the kids moving, this announcement actually stimulates certain chemicals in the brain that cause a temporary loss of hearing and mobility. We submit our own family as Exhibit A.

Each evening, we plan thirty minutes for getting the boys to bed. Plenty of time, right? Then why is it that we often require twice as much time to actually accomplish the task? You know the routine: brush teeth, go to the bathroom, read one book, read "just one more" book, say prayers, hug and kiss, drink some water, crawl into bed, get another drink of water, another hug and kiss, threaten young lives, one last hug, lights out. Whew! No wonder we run out of time and steam. The kids do all they can to avoid the inevitable, and we easily fall for their clever ploy.

To tell the truth, however, we don't really mind the hassles of bedtime because it's during our nightly routine when many precious moments occur. Some are touching, others can be quite instructive. Still others are downright funny. The trick is learning to watch for and capture these moments.

One of those instructive episodes occurred recently as I (Kurt) was reading "one last book" to Kyle, and he made a comment that hit us hard. The book included a picture of an LP record, and, upon spotting the picture, Kyle pointed and declared, "Look, Dad, a big CD!"

I realized at that moment that my son had never seen a record album, forcing me to face the stark realization that times are changing, and changing quickly. Our grade-school son had no point of reference to recognize a record album. In fact, just the other day, he asked, "Dad, can I borrow the laptop? I want to go on-line." Good grief!

That experience drove home a reality we parents must face. Technological advances are moving at a pace that staggers the imagination. But it is only one force driving a gap between what our children and we consider commonplace.

Just as "normal" is quite different for us than it was for our parents, the lenses through which our own children look at the world and interpret what they see— their worldview—will be heavily influenced by the culture around them. If the pace of change over the past three decades is any indication of things to come, it is frighten-

> .....
> ## *Music Lessons*
>
> A struggle for us has been the kind of music one of our sons listens to. Alternative music seems to be in, and I am not sure what that is. I simply say that songs that talk about sex, drugs, and getting high are in direct conflict with Scripture.
> *LK. Clovis, CA*
> .....

ing to think of what will be "normal" by the time Kyle reaches our age.

Here is the hard reality we must face as parents at the beginning of the twenty-first century: Times are changing, and not necessarily for the better. According to the "Index of Leading Cultural Indicators" compiled by Bill Bennett, the three-decade period from when we were Kyle's age to today has brought tremendous changes in the United States and beyond. Let's take a look at a few:

In the 1960s, we viewed about five hours of television per day. Today, with far more graphic and violent content, families watch more than seven hours a day. This must be why 56 percent of us believe that television has the greatest influence on our lives—more than parents, teachers and religious leaders combined!

Further breaking down family stability, divorce rates have quadrupled since 1960. There are four times as many children of broken homes today than when we were kids.

There has been a 560 percent increase in violent crime. Eight out of ten Americans will fall victim to violent crime at least once in their lives.

Three times as many children live in single-parent homes, largely because of a 400 percent increase in illegitimate births. In 1960, only 5.3 percent of all births were out-of-wedlock. By 1990, 28 percent of all births were illegitimate.

In 1972, 13 percent of pregnancies ended in abortion. By 1990, one out of four pregnancies ended with the tragedy of induced death rather than the joy of birth. During the same period of time, incidents of child abuse increased by nearly 400 percent.

The rate at which teenagers are taking their own lives has more than tripled since 1960. Today, suicide trails only accidents as the leading cause of death among adolescents.

Like it or not, we are part of a generation very different from the one our parents knew. Right and wrong no longer exist in many people's minds. (A recent Barna poll revealed that nearly 70 percent of Americans believe there is no absolute truth.) Each individual is free to create his own reality.

There is no moral consensus that serves to restrain our culture from its bent toward self-destruction. There is no purpose, no meaning, no larger "story" within which the chapters of life play a part. What is the impact of this change? Put simply, the level of competition for the hearts and minds of our children has risen dramatically.

In light of such profound cultural shift, we must become more intentional than ever about teaching our children the larger story of life. The parenting challenge is greater than it was in past generations. Living a quiet family life is no longer enough. Our kids need to be equipped to face issues few of us could have imagined only a few years ago.

We must help them understand the basic principles upon which families and individuals can build a life of lasting meaning and purpose. Common points of reference regarding truth, morality, character, faith, and other vital issues can no longer be taken for granted. We can no longer passively accept cultural norms. At times, they must be actively countered, even challenged.

Take heart! It can be done! How? By giving our kids a compass that always points true north, regardless of what direction the winds of culture are blowing at the time. We can help them establish a standard of "normal" in their lives—clearing the blur of a mixed-up world with the lenses of truth.

Off Center

Have you ever attempted to hang a picture centered on the wall? I (Kurt) usually insist that I can do so without using a measuring tape. Several misplaced holes later, I am convinced that my plan to eyeball the job has led to failure. With that "I told you so" look in her eye, Olivia hands me a measuring tape so that I can redo the job properly.

The Old Testament Book of Judges describes the tragic consequences that result when we allow our children to "eyeball" life by failing to give them an objective standard of truth. "When there was no king in Israel, everyone did what was right in his own eyes." In the absence of a godly leader, chaos ensued. Whatever suited the community at that moment was the definition of right. "If it feels good, do it!" became their motto. The people lived in total disregard to the standards of God's truth.

As a result, the people lived way off center and raised their children off center. They worshiped heathen idols, and they forgot the God who had done so much for them. As it turns out, the

Lord had to allow foreign powers to conquer and enslave His people in order to get their attention and get them back on track. Because they ignored the objective truth they were given, God had to step in and "redo the job" in order to preserve His people.

It is much easier to do it right the first time. Many parents experience unnecessary frustration and heartache due to "eyeball" parenting. But the role of Mom and Dad is too important to be treated so lightly. Our children need us to take the task seriously. They need us to clearly establish "normal" in their lives. This means setting standards based on God's rules and instilling values based on God's perspective.

Writing to believers in Rome, the Apostle Paul provided insight into the key to correcting our blurred vision, to establishing a right angle of truth in our lives.

.....

Light Fingers

Our four year old has picked up on stealing. Not that he knew he was actually stealing, but he wanted that toy or object and so he took it. We have had to sit down and explain what he did and how he would feel if someone did that to him. We also made him return the object and apologize to that person or to the parents, as well as taking his privileges away for a period of time.

C.H. Colorado Springs, CO

.....

Do not conform any longer to the pattern of this world, but be transformed by the renewing of your mind. Then you will be able to test and approve what God's will is—his good, pleasing and perfect will (Romans 12:2).

Put simply, the battle is for the mind. We have an enemy who seeks to enslave our children to lies. But we can help dispel the darkness of deception by giving our kids the light of truth. When we do, we may just begin a cycle that will last several generations.

According to Psalm 78,

He decreed statutes for Jacob and established the law in Israel,
which he commanded our forefathers to teach their children, so
the next generation would know them, even the children yet to
be born, and they in turn would tell their children. Then they
would put their trust in God and would not forget his deeds
but would keep his commands. They would not be like their
forefathers—a stubborn and rebellious generation, whose hearts
were not loyal to God, whose spirits were not faithful to him"
(vv. 5-8).

Again, we will live according to what we believe to be true, whether that belief is valid or not. Transforming the mind is a lifelong process of replacing false beliefs and perceptions with true ones. As those with the primary responsibility of shaping the perspectives of our children, we parents must understand the vital importance of giving them the corrective lenses of truth to begin with.

Bottom Line

Jesus taught that we are part of a battle in which the enemy's primary weapon is deception—which must be countered with truth. It is our job to become intentional about equipping our children with the ability to sort through the deception and recognize the truth. The Lenses Principle states that our children need the corrective lenses of truth in order to navigate the deceptive roads of life.

⤞ Chapter 4 ⤝

The Learning Principle
⤜⤞

ittle David sits between his siblings, gathered together by Mom and Dad for a ritual of scolding and boredom. He hates this part of the day. He's been told it is for his own good. But to this seven-year-old squirming ball of energy, the supposed benefits haven't yet shown themselves. Given the option, he would choose a visit to the dentist over the routine of sanctimonious torment known in his household as family devotions. Besides enduring Sunday morning sermons at church, there are few experiences less exciting in life.

If they were honest, David's parents would have to agree.

Dad would much rather be watching the game. But guilt and Mom's nudge have compelled him to force the kids to sit through his awkward presentation of a Bible lesson and prayer. He feels inadequate, ill equipped, and embarrassed as he fumbles his way through yet another chapter in the little book billed as containing "meaningful family reflections" on the faith. From the looks on the faces of his kids, they're getting about as much out of it as he is. Little Scott is picking his nose, David is staring out the window yearning to join the neighbor kids as they play hide-and-seek, and the older kids are sneaking glances at the clock wondering when this is going to end. "Yes sir," he muses, "another highly rewarding investment of time."

Mom, though pleased her husband is finally "taking spiritual leadership" in the home, wonders whether she made a mistake pushing the matter of daily devotions onto her family. The moments of lively, scriptural discussion and resulting spiritual growth she expected have yet to occur. In fact, each episode seems to reinforce her children's perception that Christianity is boring. She worries, but would never say anything to discourage Dad in his effort at spiritual training. So, with a silent smile, Mom reluctantly endures the medicine of meaningful family devotions along with the kids.

Sound familiar? Is it any wonder that so many kids who grow up in Christian homes consider the faith boring and irrelevant by the time they reach adulthood? It is unlikely this is what the Lord had in mind when he commanded us to "teach them to your children." There must be a better way.

Could it be that we have been forcing a very natural, comfortable process into a very unnatural, uncomfortable mold? Is it possible that we become frustrated with spiritual training because it was never intended to be so complicated?

Let's start with a clean sheet of paper. Erase all your preconceived notions about faith training your children. Just for a moment, forget all the guilt-driven, unpleasant attempts you've made in the past. Rather than focus on methods and activities, let's try to understand the process that is already taking place, and make it work for us rather than against us. There are several key realities we must understand before we build a plan to teach our children Christian values.

Thus far, we have examined several Scripture passages that form what we have called our theology of parenting. We have examined three principles which frame our role in teaching our children values.

The Legacy Principle: What we do today will directly influence the multi-generational cycle of family traits, beliefs, and actions—for good or bad.

The Likelihood Principle: In the context of healthy relationships, children tend to embrace the values of their parents.

The Lenses Principle: Our children need the corrective lenses of truth in order to navigate the deceptive roads of life.

The final principle in our theology of parenting may seem obvious and simplistic on the surface. But there is much we must understand behind what we call the Learning Principle.

The Learning Principle: Our children can only learn what we teach them in a manner that will reach them.

There are two important parts to this principle. First, there are things we should know about the tendencies and makeup of those that we are trying to equip—our children—if we hope to reach them. Show us a business that doesn't understand its customer, and we'll show you a business that is failing. The same is true in the context of parenting. Parents who don't understand the basic nature and character of their child are parents who are neglecting or blowing the process of spiritual training.

Second, it assumes we want them to actually learn, not just hear, what we teach. If our goal is to make an impact, we must be willing to think outside the proverbial

. . . . .

Memory Work

There was a time when our children were to learn Scripture verses for Sunday School. We'd be cramming in the car on the way to church just to get a point or an award for knowing the verse. We had to cut back on this "cramming" and just memorize what we could handle. This made a tremendous difference in our children's memorization achievement.

C.W., Brush Prairie, WA

. . . . .

box in order to engage their hearts and minds. As we will discover, there are three windows of opportunity every parent has with his or her child. Depending upon which of these windows your child is in, your approach to training him or her will differ. The best intentions will still miss the mark if we are aiming at the wrong target.

Let's begin with an overview of what the Scriptures tell us about the nature and character of children.

A Theology of Your Child

As we examine this final principle in our theology of parenting, we must briefly examine what might be called a theology of your child. God has given an owner's manual for the human personality. As parents, we can glean from the Bible answers to several fundamental questions about human nature, and in the process, take some of the mystery out of raising children.

As we examine the Scriptures, we will discover good news and bad news about the condition of our children. The good news is that, as part of the human family, your child is made in the image of God. Consequently, he or she possesses some wonderful, awe-inspiring qualities. The bad news is that, as part of the human family, your child has a fallen, sinful nature. Consequently, he or she possesses some destructive, terrible qualities. We must understand both realities and allow them to inform our role as parents. Let's begin with the good news.

The Good News

In the opening scene of the Bible, we are given reason to be optimistic about the character of our children. We discover that "God created man in his own image, in the image of God he created him; male and female he created them" (Genesis 1:27).

Most Christians have heard that, as originally designed, man was created in the likeness of the Creator Himself. But what does it really mean? Do we mirror His physical likeness? Actually, as a spirit, God does not have parts like a man. Rather, it means that we have a mental, moral, and social likeness, granting us the qualities and capacities that make us truly human.

In His mental likeness, we are able to reason and exercise our will. We are more than robotic computers, programmed to predetermined ends. We can think and choose. Animals are driven by instinctive urges. Humans can be guided by reasoned choices.

In His moral likeness, we have a conscience. God is holy and compelled by His very nature to resist evil. In similar fashion, we are not morally passive, but are able to distinguish what is right from what is wrong, what is good from what is bad. Animals are driven by what feels good. Humans can know and choose what is right.

In His social likeness, we are able to love and relate to others. God has a social nature which motivated Him to create and love man. In like manner, we seek companionship, yearning to love and be loved by God and others. Animals can respond to others. Humans are able to truly love others.

Just as adults are made after the likeness of God, so are our children, and they possess some wonderful, awe-inspiring qualities.

The Bad News

Now for the bad news. The second scene of Genesis. You know the story. After giving access to and dominion over everything on earth, God placed one restriction on Adam—not to eat from the tree of the knowledge of good and evil. The tempter came. The trap was set. The bait was offered. The sin was committed. Man broke the law, and the heart of his Creator. The deceiver stole the heart of God's beloved. The human race chose the path of pain over the path of perfection.

How does the sin of Adam and Eve impact our children?

Remember the Principle of Legacy? It tells us that our actions today will impact future generations. As our first ancestors, Adam and Eve made a choice that has impacted every child born into the human race—including yours. As the Apostle Paul writes several hundred generations later,

> *For all have sinned and fall short of the glory of God* (Romans 3:23).

> *Therefore, just as sin entered the world through one man, and death through sin, and in this way death came to all men, because all sinned . . .* (Romans 5:12).

The harsh truth we must face is that our children were not born with an innocent nature, prone toward good, but rather with a sinful nature, prone toward evil. The Principle of Legacy impacted our children long before any of us were born. Our kids have the same disease as the rest of us—sin.

Implications

The realities of human nature that form our theology of children also inform our theology of parenting. Drawing upon their truths, we can glean several implications for the process of teaching our children values.

Reality #1: Children have a rational, free will which gives them the capacity to understand and choose what is right, but because of a sinful nature, they will tend to choose what is wrong. Implication: We can hold our children responsible for their choices, teaching them to counter their natural impulses, rather than encourage or excuse them.

Reality #2: Children have a conscience with which to distinguish right from wrong, but can become callous to its urgings. Implication: We must help them develop and maintain an informed, sensitive conscience by clarifying right from wrong, truth from error.

Reality #3: Children have an inborn yearning for relationship with God and others, but will resist and resent His or any other authority. Implication: We should expect resistance to our authority and instruction, and find ways to push past the surface rebellion in order to tap the deeper yearning.

Reality #4: Children are born with inherent worth and dignity, with tremendous capacity for good or evil. Implication: We should balance unconditional love for their person with conditional acceptance of behavior.

To summarize, our children have been created in the likeness of God Himself, giving them tremendous potential and awe-inspiring qualities. But due to the Fall, they are prone toward evil and deception. Our job as parents is to understand the implications of these realities as we seek to teach them Christian values.

.....

Family Night Wrangle

Family nights were daunting to me. I had to try to get both children in my presence, and they were arguing when around each other. Also, my youngest taunted me and attempted to redirect me with anger. When I dropped the formality of the attempt to implement family nights and grabbed any opportunity to create a "teachable moment" instead, it began to improve. Then, to my surprise, my toughest critic asked me one day, "Mom when are we going to do a family night?"

JJ, Clovis, CA

.....

Ages and Stages _____

For nearly fifteen years, Kurt has had the privilege of working with Dr. James Dobson, founder and president of Focus on the Family. Much of that time has been spent assisting Dr. Dobson with the thousands of letters and phone calls he receives each month seeking advice and asking questions on every imaginable aspect of family life. Of course, spiritual training of children is one of the issues consistently raised as parents wonder whether or not they should allow children to "decide for themselves" on matters of faith. Dr. Dobson's answer (reprinted here from the book *Solid Answers*) provides insight into the windows of a child's maturation.

Shortly after [a gosling] hatches from his shell he will become attached, or "imprinted," to the first thing that he sees moving near him. From that time forward, the gosling follows that particular object when it moves in his vicinity. Ordinarily, it becomes imprinted to the mother goose who was on hand to hatch the new generation.

Time is the critical factor in this process. The gosling is vulnerable to imprinting for only a few seconds after it hatches from the shell; if that opportunity is lost, it cannot be regained later. In other words, there is a brief "critical period" in the life of a gosling when this instinctual learning is possible. . . .

There is also a critical period when certain kinds of instruction are easier in the life of children. Although humans have no instincts (only drives, reflexes, urges, etc.) there is a brief period during childhood when youngsters are vulnerable to religious training. Their concepts of right and wrong are formulated during this time, and their view of God begins to solidify. As in the case of the gosling, the opportunity of that period must be seized when it is available. . . . When parents withhold indoctrination from their small children, allowing them to "decide for themselves," the adults are almost guaranteeing that their youngsters will "decide" in the negative. If parents want their children to have a meaningful faith, they must give up any misguided attempts at objectivity. . . .

After the middle-adolescent age (ending at about fifteen years), children sometimes resent heavy-handedness about anything—including what to believe. But if the early exposure has been properly conducted, they should have an anchor to steady them. Their early indoctrination, then, is the key to the spiritual attitudes they carry into adulthood.[1]

We cannot teach a six-year-old child in the same way that we teach a fourteen year old. They are in different stages of development and openness. Priorities change as they mature, making it vital that we understand each stage of development if we are going to create an intentional plan for teaching them Christian values in a manner that will reach them.

Dorothy Sayers, a colleague of C.S. Lewis, presented an insightful paper at Oxford University in 1947 entitled "The Lost Tools of Learning." In it, she described a framework for academic training that is consistent with the classical model called the Trivium. The Trivium consisted of three parts: grammar, dialectic, and rhetoric. When a child successfully passed these three programs, he was equipped for specialization in the academic discipline of choice. In essence, the Trivium taught a person how to learn before he entered the rigors of advanced, specialized academic study.

The first stage, grammar, involved memorizing basic facts. Young children love to chant, recite, and memorize. Thus, stage one aligned with the first phase of childhood development.

The second stage, dialectic, involved the study of logic and argumentation. Older children and pre-teens love to argue and debate. Thus, stage two aligned with the second major phase of childhood development by teaching how to argue and debate properly.

The third stage, rhetoric, involved learning how to articulate what one thinks. Teens are coming of age, forming their own view of the world. Thus, stage three aligned with the third and final phase of childhood by helping them express the ideas they've adopted in a clear, effective manner.

In his excellent book on classical education entitled *Recovering the Lost Tools of Learning*, Douglas Wilson comments on the benefits of this framework for learning.

> *When grammar, dialectic, and rhetoric are taught at these ages, the teacher is teaching "with the grain." Two things are accomplished. The children enjoy what they do, and what they do equips them with the tools of learning.* [2]

The thousands of parents and educators who have adopted Sayers' framework for instruction are consistently demonstrating the power of the Learning Principle.

> *Family Night Activity*
>
> I have found that Family Tool Chest workbooks are helpful for training children. It isn't necessarily the message, but the ability to relate the message to a fun and even silly activity that brings the point home. My daughter even created her own family night activity. We came into her room, shut the door and the curtains, and turned out all of the lights. Then she turned on a flashlight and explained to us that the flashlight is like God showing us what to do when we can't see where to go.
>
> *D.H. Colorado Springs, CO*

Because children are being taught in a manner consistent with their specific window of development, they learn much better.

We have identified three windows of opportunity in the lives of our children for spiritual and values training—the imprint period, the impression period, and the coaching period. Each requires a different approach to instruction based upon the developmental stage of the child. Obviously, specific ages will vary with each child, and our role as parent-teachers changes as our children pass from the imprint period to the impression period, and finally into the coaching period.

Imprint Period *(Age seven and under)* _____

The Imprint Period is the window of development in which children are all ears. They listen. Young children want to know what Mom and Dad think in order to know what they think. Like the gosling described earlier, they are eager to line up behind Mom or Dad—accepting without much question our values and beliefs. We must be diligent during this window of opportunity because it passes quickly.

What and how we teach during the imprint period should align with the bent of younger children. They love games, stories, songs, memorization, and other activities that can be used as powerful tools in the process of teaching them Christian beliefs and values.

Impression Period *(Age Eight to Fourteen)* _____

In general, children from eight to fourteen years are in a second window called the Impression Period. The days are gone when they accepted whatever we said without question. But they are still highly impressionable—open to our direction and influence. They ask questions, wanting to know the why along with the what. "Because I say so!" doesn't cut it any longer. Trying to sort through a vast universe of information and make sense of it all, they need our guidance through the process.

What and how we teach during this second period should change to be consistent with a new stage of development. Children in the impression period want to know what we believe, but they also want help to understand the rationale behind those beliefs. They want to debate (a.k.a. argue) what we teach. We should see this trend as positive, not negative. They have outgrown blind acceptance. Our job is to help them learn to think for themselves.

Coaching Period (Over Fourteen) _____

By the time our children reach approximately fifteen years of age, the window of influence is closing. They are approaching adulthood and must be allowed to form their own opinions and values. The goal of our investment during the imprint and impression stages is to equip them to make their own choices in an informed, mature manner. At this point, however, our role transitions from teacher to coach.

A good coach recognizes that athletes must be allowed to make and learn from mistakes. Coaches get players ready for the game; they don't play the game for them. When our kids enter the coaching period, our job changes. We can motivate, encourage, challenge, and advise. But we can't force feed. We can help them learn to articulate what they believe. We can challenge their thinking. We can remind them of the "basics" they learned during the "practices" of the imprint and impression periods. We can give them a safe environment to wrestle with, even question, the values we've taught them. But we can't—we must not—treat them as if they are still in the imprint or impression periods.

When we reach the coaching period, we can't "wing it" when it comes to spiritual training. Pat answers won't cut it. We must be willing to wrestle with the tough issues right along with our teenage children, making every effort to be informed ourselves, searching out and finding resources that can address difficult questions in an honest, authentic, and credible manner. Again, a good coach may not have all the answers, but knows which way to point.

Impression Points _____

Regardless of which of the three windows of development our children are in, the key to effective parenting is intentionality. The better we understand our children, the better equipped we will be to teach them in a manner that will reach them. How? By learning to create and capture opportunities to impress our beliefs and values in their lives.

Israel was on the precipice. Their future was set. God had led them to the Promised Land and was ready to pour the sweetness of possessions into their lives. In a final debriefing session, God instructed Moses to lay out a very clear discourse to help the people cope with the success that was awaiting. His instructions went like this.

Love the Lord your God with all your heart and with all your soul and with all your strength. These commandments that I give you today are to be upon your hearts. IMPRESS them on your children!

How?

Talk about them when you sit at home and when you walk along the road, when you lie down and when you get up. Tie them as symbols on your hands and bind them on your foreheads. Write them on the doorframes of your houses and on your gates (Deuteronomy 6:5-9).

God was on the verge of giving His people a large land with ready-made cities. He would provide houses filled with good things, water wells they wouldn't have to dig, crops they didn't plant. He knew they would be filled to satisfaction. He also knew the dangers. Possessions tend to consume our attention . . . houses, wells, farms. . . . They require constant care, endless improvements, and time-consuming upkeep. The implication shouting at us between the lines is that when we get really busy . . . when we become "satisfied" . . . our relationship with God seems to become less important, our relationship with the children suffers, and our diligence wanes. We start to neglect the process of teaching the next generation about what is truly important. So, in order to keep us on track, God commanded His people to create and capitalize upon what we have labeled "impression points."

They happen every day of our lives. We impress upon the children our values, preferences, quirks, and concerns. We do it through our talk and our walk. We do it intentionally, and we do it incidentally. Sometimes we turn them on to our ideas. Other times we just turn them off. Those who are able to make impression points work for them, rather than against them, have mastered a very powerful art. The first step in doing so is understanding what they are and how they work.

In short, impression points are those times in life when we make an impression upon our children—when we "impress" them with who we are, what we think, or what we do. They can be intentionally created or they can incidentally occur. Either way, they make an impression . . . for good or bad.

The Learning Principle says that our children will only learn what we teach them in a manner that will reach them. Impression points are the method for reaching them. Those described in Deuteronomy are both intentional and incidental in nature. Intentional impression points are those we create; they are planned. Incidental impression points, on the other hand, just happen. They occur in the everyday of life, and they happen whether we are ready for them or not. Our job is to recognize such occasions and capitalize on the moment.

The key word related to impression points is "creating." Incidental impression points are often birthed by the intentional. A formal event often sets up informal conversation, and it is the informal that has a more lasting impact. One intentionally created impression point can spawn a host of incidentals. But first, someone must take the time to purposefully plan the intentional impressions. In the chapters to follow, we will walk you through a plan and share some great ideas for doing just that.

Bottom Line _____

There are two things we need to know about our children as we
seek to teach them Christian values. First, we must understand
their basic nature. They are created in the image of God with
tremendous capacity for good, but they are part of a fallen race,
resulting in a bent toward evil. Second, we need to know whether
they are in the imprint, impression, or coaching period in order to
tailor our teaching efforts to their stage of development.

With this knowledge, we are better equipped to implement
the Learning Principle, which states that our children can only
learn what we teach them in a manner that will reach them.
Toward this end, Deuteronomy 6 commands us to create and
capture "impression points" in the everyday of life.

PART 2

Compass Beliefs

⇥ Chapter 5 ⇤

Who Is God?

A third-grade teacher once gave her students a writing assignment to explain God. Here is a portion of one response from eight-year-old Danny Dutton.

One of God's main jobs is making people. He makes these to put in place of the ones that die so there will be enough people to care for things here on earth. He doesn't make grown-ups. Just babies. I think because they are smaller and easier to make. That way he doesn't have to take up his valuable time teaching them to talk and walk. He can just leave that up to the mothers and fathers. I think it works out pretty good.

God's second most important job is listening to prayers. An awful lot of this goes on, as some people, like preachers and things pray other times besides bedtime. Grandpa and Grandma pray every time they eat—except for snacks.

Atheists are people who don't believe in God. I don't think there are any in my city. At least there aren't any who come to our church. They have their own church.

Jesus is God's Son. He used to do all the hard work like walking on water and doing miracles. They finally got tired of

Him preaching to them and they cursified Him. His Dad (God) appreciated everything He had done on earth, so He told Him He didn't have to go out on the road anymore. He could stay in heaven. So He did. And now He helps His Dad out by listening to prayers and seeing which things are important for God to take care of and which ones He can take care of Himself without having to bother God with it. You can pray anytime you want and they're sure to hear you because they've got it worked out so one of them is on duty all the time.

If you don't believe in God, besides being an atheist, you will be very lonely . . . because your parents can't go everywhere with you like to camp, but God can. I figure God put me here and He can take me back anytime He pleases and that's why I believe in God.

Lightning Show

We were watching an amazing lightning storm from a screened-in porch. Our four-year-old son asked, "Wouldn't it be great if God made lightening in color?" We got the chance to discuss God's creativity.

T.B. Colorado Springs, CO

It is apparent that someone has attempted to give Danny Dutton a basic understanding of the biblical view of God. He may not have every detail right, but he is well on his way to understanding one of the most important realities of life—the reality and character of God.

What to Understand

The basis of a Christian worldview is the belief in the God of the Bible. In order to identify true north with regard to the reality and character of God, the following should be understood.

Importance: We live in an era in which there are many different views of God. In addition to the major world religions, individuals often develop their own view of God based upon personal preference rather than revealed truth. Therefore, we must help establish "normal" for our kids by teaching them the Christian view of God, equipping them to recognize truth from error.

Compass Belief: There is one God. He is the perfect Spirit in whom all things have their source, support, and end. He is a personal being, not an impersonal force. He is just and loving, and cares about you and me.

Supporting Scriptures: The following passages describe key aspects of the reality and character of God.

THERE IS ONE GOD

Hear, O Israel: The Lord our God, the Lord is one (Deuteronomy 6:4).

HE IS A SPIRIT

God is spirit, and his worshipers must worship in spirit and in truth (John 4:24).

HE IS THE SOURCE OF EVERYTHING

Through him all things were made; without him nothing was made that has been made (John 1:3).
"Who has ever given to God, that God should repay him?"
For from him and through him and to him are all things. To him be the glory forever! Amen (Romans 11:35-36).

HE IS A PERSON

The Lord was grieved that he had made man on the earth, and his heart was filled with pain (Genesis 6:6).
Do not worship any other god, for the Lord, whose name is Jealous, is a jealous God (Exodus 34:14).
(Note: An impersonal force can't grieve, hurt, or be jealous.)

HE IS HOLY AND JUST

*I am the Lord your God; consecrate yourselves and be holy,
because I am holy* (Leviticus 11:44a).
*God "will give to each person according to what he has
done." For God does not show favoritism* (Romans 2:6, 11).

HE IS LOVING

*For God so loved the world that he gave his one and only
Son, that whoever believes in him shall not perish but have
eternal life* (John 3:16).
Cast all your anxiety on him because he cares for you
(1 Peter 5:7).
*This is love: not that we loved God, but that he loved us and
sent his Son as an atoning sacrifice for our sins* (1 John
4:10).

Impression Points _____

Following are several ideas for teaching the reality and character
of God to children of various ages. Pick and choose the impression
points that will work best for your family.

Real Life Moments

God's Character: When our children are very small (1-3), we
imprint their lives by how we treat them rather than by instruc-
tional activities. It is in this season that we impress their hearts,
not their heads. Because children form their early view of God
largely from how they view their parents, we can use the early
years to reinforce the character of God—including both His love
and His justice.

Love: When our children are very small, the best way to
impress the love of God upon their hearts is by doing what
comes naturally. We should overwhelm them with affirma-
tion and affection—including lots of hugs and kisses, and
praise for their fledgling attempts to talk, walk, and feed

themselves. In these small ways, we are demonstrating unconditional love and the kind of affection God has for us. (By the way, don't stop as the child ages!)

Justice: In addition to establishing the security of unconditional love and affection when our children are very small, it is important to establish a clear sense that Mom and Dad set the rules and that the child is expected to obey those rules. Starting at about eighteen months, establish a consistent system of discipline for times your child willfully defies your rules. We demonstrate God's character when we refuse to tolerate rebellion against the rules we've established. Please note, however, that there is a difference between willful defiance and childish irresponsibility. Like God, we must clarify right from wrong with children and bring about appropriate discipline when the standard is violated. Parents who neglect this principle during the early years risk giving children the mistaken idea that love and justice are mutually exclusive. God is both, and we must model both. Some excellent resources to help you implement this balance include *Dare To Discipline* and *Hide or Seek,* both written by Dr. James Dobson.

Planned Activities

Just Like Air: Five-year-old Kyle and three-year-old Shaun stare at Dad seriously, contemplating his rather deep question. "How could God be real if we can't see Him?"

The oldest takes the lead. "That's a good question, Dad!"

"Well, is there anything else we know is real but we can't see?" asks Dad.

"How about air?" suggests Mom.

Dad pulls out several balloons. He inflates them.

"Air is real enough to expand these balloons. I bet air has power too," Dad says while releasing his balloon. Now Shaun, the three year old, is really engaged! After ten minutes of intense competition over who can make his balloons fly farthest, Dad introduces a little slogan for tonight's activity. "Just like air, God is there!"

A lasting impression was made. In fact, ask the boys about how God can be real even though we can't see Him, and they will immediately respond, "Just like air, God is there!" Ask them what that means, and they'll explain, "God is real and has power, even though we can't see Him." (Ages 3–8)

God Is Everywhere: Observing the beauty outside the car window while driving down the freeway, I (Kurt) asked my then five-year-old son where God lives. Disturbed by Dad's lack of theological education, he quickly and confidently responded with, "He lives everywhere, Dad!"

"How can He live everywhere if He is just one person?" I asked, pushing beyond the acceptable rules of father/son interaction. After thinking for a long moment, he threw the ball back into my court.

"I don't know, Dad. You'll have to teach me about that one!"

Realizing it was now necessary to develop an activity that would teach the omnipresence and omniscience of God at a five-year-old level, I was sorry I ever raised the topic. But we came up with a few simple activities that seemed to do the trick.

Hide and Seek: Every child loves to play hide and seek with his parents. This simple game can be used to illustrate the truth taught in Psalm 139:7-10, that we cannot hide from God because He is everywhere and knows everything. After reading the passage in a children's version of the Bible, play hide and seek with your children. When someone is found, yell out the phrase, "You can't hide from God!" This will reinforce the truth in your child's mind. Your child will want to do this each time you play hide and seek. (Ages 3–8)

Picture Parable: Young children love to draw and color.

You can use a simple drawing to illustrate the reality that God is everywhere at once because He is outside the limits of time and space. Take some paper and crayons and ask your child to draw a picture of the world. Next, have him draw a picture of himself and a good friend inside that world. Ask the question, "Can you see (insert name of friend) right now?" Answer—no. "Why not?" Answer— because he/she is in another house with walls between us. Instruct the child to draw a wall between the two characters on the picture to show that they can't see one another. Ask the question, "When you look down at the world that you made, can you see yourself and your friend?" Answer—yes. That is the way God sees the entire world. He can see everyone even though we can't see each other. (Ages 4–6)

God Made All Things: After reading the Creation story in a children's picture Bible, pull out a large box of linking toys such as Legos or Connects. Help the kids make several designs, such as people or cars or houses. After completing the "creation" process, take the creations apart and place the individual pieces on the floor. Ask, "How long do you think it will take for these pieces to put themselves back together without any help from us?"

The obvious answer: It will never happen.

Next, take the toy pieces and place them all in a bag or box. Ask the children to shake the bag or box around and then dump them on the floor. After the pieces fall randomly, express frustration.

"I wanted them to fall into place to re-create the same designs we made before! Why didn't it work?" Try again over and over and keep expressing frustration that it doesn't work.

The kids will consider you silly, which is precisely what you want!

Pose the question, "How many times do you think it will take shaking and dumping before they become the designs again?"

The obvious answer: It will never happen.

Explain that many people believe that the world simply made itself by chance rather than that God created it on purpose. Just as you were silly to expect the toys to fall into place, it is silly to think our entire world made itself without a Creator! (Ages 4–9)

Field Trips

Romans One Field Trips: The first chapter of Romans (vv. 18-20) says that God has made His nature and character evident from the things He has made—including His eternal power and divine nature. As parents, we can turn routine outings into opportunities to highlight various aspects of God's nature with our children. A trip to the zoo, for example, can be used to discover God's marvelous creativity and sense of humor. A hiking trip can become an examination of the brilliant engineering behind ecological systems—working together to sustain life in all shapes and sizes. Moments of a ski trip can be captured to intentionally experience God's eye for beauty as you take in the masterpiece of mountain-top views. The key is commenting on such moments in order to turn them into "Romans One Field Trips." (All ages)

Dinner Table Debate

A great way to help our children better grasp and defend what they believe is to create "dinner table debates." Set the day you plan to hold your debate during dinner, assigning different sides of the issue to individuals or teams. (For example, Mom and son defend the existence of God while Dad and daughter oppose it.) Give the teams several days or weeks to prepare for the debate. When the big day arrives, remind everyone to bring his or her notes and be prepared to begin the debate immediately after asking the blessing. It is wise to assign a moderator or to clearly establish rules for the debate in order to keep everything fair and in control.

If you choose to use dinner table debates in your family, consider several important points. First, you may be concerned about seriously entertaining arguments which oppose your beliefs. However, it is better for your children to struggle with these issues in the safety and spirit of a believing home than to be exposed to these ideas in a less supportive context. Second, this requires some work on the part of the parents. You must be willing to learn along with your kids, including taking the time to read and prepare. It may do more harm than good to organize a debate in which you can't engage. Helpful resources to obtain in preparing for a debate on the existence of God include the following.

Does God Exist: The Great Debate by J.P. Moreland and Kai Nielsen (Thomas Nelson: 1990).

Know What You Believe by Paul Little—A popular, introductory level book on systematic theology. Covers such topics as the Bible, God, Jesus Christ, man and sin, etc.

Know Why You Believe by Paul Little—A popular, introductory level text on apologetics. Covers such questions as "Is Christianity rational?" "Did Christ rise from the dead?" etc.

. . . . .

Conversation Cues

Recently after a soccer practice my wife and I were talking about the team. My daughter jumped into the conversation with a less than flattering observation about one of her teammates. We realized that we had probably given a cue for my daughter to make such a comment, so we changed the conversation to talk about the strong points of all the players and the importance of encouraging one another and building up our friends and teammates.

D.H. Colorado Springs, CO

. . . . .

Entertainment
Movie Night: As you enjoy watching movies with older kids, capture the moment and reflect upon how certain films or scenes within a film reflect a view of God either consistent or inconsistent with a Christian perspective. (Of course, you must carefully decide what films are age- and content-appropriate for your children.) Several films which create such opportunities include the following.

Dead Poet's Society: In this film, the main character, Mr. Keating (played by Robin Williams), reflects a view of the world which says that we should pursue life to the fullest while we are alive because when it is over, it's over. The primary theme is "Carpe Diem—Seize the Day!" The film ends in tragedy for a boy named Neil because he is unable to get from life what he wants, so he kills himself. After viewing the film, ask the following discussion questions.

Question: What view of God does Robin Williams' character represent? Answer: The view that there is no God—or at least there is no life beyond this life.

Question: What book of the Bible speaks to the same issue? Answer: The Book of Ecclesiastes because it talks about what life is like without God.

Question: Why did the boy kill himself? Answer: Because he thought there was no meaning to life unless he could do what he wanted with his life.

Question: Why is this a lie? Answer: Because the truth is that there is a God who gives us purpose and meaning, even when life doesn't go as we want it to.

Contact: In this film, the main character (played by Jodie Foster) is a scientist on a quest to find intelligent life beyond earth. Once contact is made, the people of earth create a machine which allows her to travel across the galaxies and communicate directly with alien beings. There is a scene in the film where the main character is traveling through space and becomes overwhelmed with the beauty and majesty of space—to the point that she can't even speak. Zero in on this scene and ask the following discussion questions.

Question: What view of God does Jodie Foster's character represent? Answer: The view that without proof, we can't believe in God

Question: Why did she become overwhelmed at the splendor and majesty of space? Answer: Because she was experiencing something greater than herself.

Question: What passage of Scripture speaks to what she experienced while traveling through space? Answer: Psalm 19 says that the heavens declare the glory of God!

Question: What is the truth she refused to accept? Answer: That the order and beauty of our universe is evidence of a Creator God.

Drive Time or Bedtime Audios

Driving our kids from school to soccer practice to church activities to who knows where doesn't need to be wasted time. Neither do long vacation drive times, which create ideal opportunities to enjoy a good speech, drama, or book on tape addressing the issues we are trying to teach our children. The most well-known and effective tools for this purpose are the "Adventures in Odyssey" radio drama tapes produced by Focus on the Family. Here are some specific episodes that deal with the theme of God's nature and character. (Note: You can call Focus on the Family at 1-800-232-6459 to request the individual cassettes by name or episode number and find out whether the episode you need is packaged within a larger album.) (Ages 6–12)

"Hallowed Be Thy Name" (Adventures in Odyssey "AIO" episode #231)

"Greater Love" (AIO episode #224)
"Bernard and Joseph" (AIO episode #130 & #131)
"Our Daily Bread" (AIO episode #234)
"Thy Will Be Done" (AIO episode #233)

Reading Rewards

One of the most important areas in which we help our children form their view of the world is by providing them with quality reading material. Establish a reading reward system which gives an incentive to your children for reading books (or having books read to them) which either reinforce or challenge their thinking on key beliefs. For example, you may wish to pay them an appropriate amount of money for every book on your list they read, or earn points toward some special outing, or whatever incentive will work for your child. In order to instill a love for reading and find titles appropriate for this and other topics, we recommend that you obtain several resources such as the following.

Honey for a Child's Heart by Gladys Hunt—This book is one of the best guides to children's books available. It is for parents looking for guidance in the pursuit of good literature for their kids.

The Sonlight Curriculum Catalog—This catalog for home schooling lists hundreds of books with descriptions by grade-appropriate levels. A copy can be obtained by calling 303-730-6292, or visit their web site at www.sonlight-curriculum.com.

The Read-Aloud Handbook by Jim Trelease—This book includes a giant treasury of great read-aloud books and coaches parents on how to instill a love for reading in children.

These ideas, as those in other chapters, are given as suggestions to get your own creative juices going. The key is that you begin to intentionally create and capture opportunities to point the family compass toward truth.

❧ *Chapter 6* ❧

Is the Devil Real?

*I*n the preface to his classic book *The Screwtape Letters*,
C.S. Lewis makes an important observation for all to consider as
they seek to understand Satan and his demons.

> *There are two equal and opposite errors into which our race
> can fall about the devils. One is to disbelieve in their existence.
> The other is to believe, and to feel an excessive and unhealthy
> interest in them. They themselves are equally pleased by both
> errors, and hail a materialist or a magician with the same
> delight.*[1]

If we ignore the reality of Satan, we will fail to perceive his
deceptions. If we are obsessed with the Devil and his ways, we
can fall into unnecessary fear, or worse, unhealthy exploration.
Our children need to be equipped to avoid either error by
learning what the Bible teaches as true about the enemy of
our souls—Satan.

What to Understand

A second key component to a Christian worldview is understanding the reality of and person behind evil. In order to identify true north with regard to the ways and work of Satan, the following should be understood.

Importance: Most people in our generation fall into either extreme of disbelief in or unhealthy obsession with the devil. Some see evil in the world but find it hard to believe that a little guy in a red suit and pointed tail is the mastermind behind it all. Others become obsessed with the seductive lure of evil or fearful of the mystical forces of demons to the point that they elevate Satan above his rightful place. Therefore, we must help our children establish "normal" by teaching them the biblical view of Satan and his work in the world.

Compass Belief: The devil was an angel created to serve God with many wonderful gifts. But he rebelled against God, led other angels to rebel against God, and hopes to get people to join his rebellion. He hates us and seeks to destroy our souls through temptation and lies. Satan and all who follow him will be judged by God!

Supporting Scriptures: The following passages describe key aspects of the reality and work of Satan.

SATAN IS AN ANGEL WHO REBELLED

How you have fallen from heaven, O morning star, son of the dawn! You have been cast down to the earth, you who once laid low the nations! You said in your heart, "I will ascend to heaven; I will raise my throne above the stars of God; I will sit enthroned on the mount of assembly, on the utmost heights of the sacred mountain. I will ascend above the tops of the clouds; I will make myself like the Most High." But you are brought down to the grave, to the depths of the pit (Isaiah 14:12-15). *"You were the model of perfection, full of wisdom and perfect in beauty. . . . You were anointed as a guardian cherub, for so I ordained you. . . . You were blameless in your ways from the day you were created till wickedness was found in you. . . . So I drove you in disgrace from the mount of God, and I expelled you, O guardian cherub. . . . Your heart became proud on account of your beauty, and you corrupted your wisdom because of your splendor. So I threw you to the earth"* (Ezekiel 28:12-17).

SATAN IS AN ENEMY WHO WANTS TO DESTROY US

Put on the full armor of God so that you can take your stand against the devil's schemes. For our struggle is not against flesh and blood, but against the rulers, against the authorities, against the powers of this dark world and against the spiritual forces of evil in the heavenly realms (Ephesians 6:11-12).

Be self-controlled and alert. Your enemy the devil prowls around like a roaring lion looking for someone to devour (1 Peter 5:8).

SATAN IS A TEMPTER AND LIAR

Then Jesus was led by the Spirit into the desert to be tempted by the devil (Matthew 4:1-11).

You belong to your father, the devil, and you want to carry out your father's desire. He was a murderer from the beginning, not holding to the truth, for there is no truth in him. When he lies, he speaks his native language, for he is a liar and the father of lies (John 8:44).

Satan himself masquerades as an angel of light (2 Corinthians 11:14).

SATAN WILL BE JUDGED

And the devil, who deceived them, was thrown into the lake of burning sulfur, where the beast and the false prophet had been thrown. They will be tormented day and night forever and ever (Revelation 20:10).

Impression Points _____

Following are several ideas for teaching the reality and work of Satan to children of various ages. Pick and choose the impression points that will work best for your family.

Real Life Moments

Danger: One of the unpleasant tasks we have as parents is helping our children understand from an early age that there are evil people in the world who would hurt us if they had a chance. So, we tell them to be careful of strangers, to stay close to Mommy or Daddy while in public, to tell us if someone touches them where they shouldn't, etc. Whether or not you choose to overtly describe the Devil in this context, these necessary occasions can serve to introduce your younger children to the existence of an enemy present in the world.

Good Guys, Bad Guys: Children naturally play pretend games which include good guys and bad guys. Some parents find this troubling. However, it is another opportunity to reinforce in the minds of our younger children that there are forces of good and forces of evil which oppose one another. These forces are led by two persons—God and Satan. Depending upon the ages of your children, you may wish to use the image of "good guys and bad guys" to illustrate the story of Satan's rebellion. Satan turned

.....

Monster Stories

Our seven year old comes home with stories he has heard from a classmate who talks about monsters and witches living in everyone's houses and closets. We have plenty of opportunities to talk about God and what the Bible says about these ideas. Also, we talk about making right choices when friends make choices that are not so right. We think it's important to know why certain choices are wrong and what should have been done instead.

S.K. Clovis, CA

.....

against God and has been recruiting others to oppose God, including angels and people.

Planned Activities
Satan Fools: Kids get a kick out of playing practical jokes on people. Take advantage of this urge by creating an activity that highlights the fact that Satan loves to trick and deceive us. Be sure to explain clearly that the jokes we play on one another are done out of love, are intended for fun, and should never hurt another person or property, while the trickery of the Devil is intended to hurt us.

Help your children plan and pull off several practical jokes to play on Mom, Dad, or siblings. Here are some possible examples.

Offer someone a piece of candy by extending your hand. Just as she is about to grab it, pull your hand away and say, "Fooled ya!"

Prop a pillow atop a slightly opened bedroom door. Call for Dad (or someone else) to come into the bedroom to see something. When he opens the door all the way and the pillow falls onto his head, say, "Fooled ya!"

Posture as if you want to give Mom (or someone else) a loving hug. While embracing, drop a piece of ice down her back and say, "Fooled ya!"

Turn off the lights and use a flashlight and a toy (or paper cutout) to create a scary shadow on the wall. Invite Mom (or someone else) to come into the room. Mom should act frightened, giving the kids the opportunity to say, "Fooled ya!"

Read John 8:44 and point out that the Devil is a liar, meaning that he seeks to fool us into believing what is not true. Just as the practical jokes tricked us into thinking one thing when something else was true, so Satan's schemes are designed to fool us into thinking one thing when something else is true. Read James 4:7 and point out that by submitting to God (and His truth) we can resist the devil (and his lies). You may want to cap the activity with the saying, "God rules, Satan fools!" (Ages 5–9)

Traps: An excellent way to teach children about how Satan works is to use common traps. When you have that occasional mouse in your home, ask your kids to help you set the trap. Use the opportunity to discuss what Ephesians 6:11 describes as the "schemes" or "snares" of Satan. You may wish to go further by planning an activity in which your children set various traps and watch how they catch their prey. Again, the goal is to help the children understand that Satan will use what we like (the cheese, etc.) to lure us in and trap us because his true goal is to kill and destroy as stated in 1 Peter 5:8. (Ages 5-10)

Armor of God: Little boys love to play with toy armor and pretend to be soldiers. This is a great opportunity to teach how the Bible tells us to put on the armor of God in order to stand against the schemes of the devil. Read through Ephesians 6:10-18 together. As each piece of armor is described, stop to make the belt of truth, breastplate of righteousness, shield of faith, etc. out of cardboard or other supplies. Describe the kinds of things Satan does to defeat us, and why we need both defensive and offensive weapons to win the spiritual battle against God's enemy. You may also want to obtain the "Full Armor of God Play Set" from Rainfall toys to play with as an ongoing approach to reinforcing the lesson of this activity.

Field Trip

Media Outing: Much of today's music and other popular media clearly reflect the realities of spiritual warfare. In fact, many stars overtly and unapologetically promote occultic or satanic messages and themes. For older kids, take a field trip to the local media store and look at CD covers, song titles, movie and computer game themes, book topics, magazine emphasis, etc. Identify several promoting satanic themes and ask the following questions.

Question: What do these products tell us about the spiritual war going on around us as described in Ephesians 6:11-12? Answer: They show that we are in a spiritual battle, and that Satan's forces are using the media very effectively.

Question: Do you think these artists are ashamed of what they believe? Answer: Not at all. They are proud and overt about what they believe.

> .....
>
> ## Repentance
>
> One night when our daughter was nine, I heard sobbing coming from her room after she had gone to bed. I went in, sat down, and listened. She had said some unkind things at school and her "heart hurt." We discussed repentance, forgiveness, and restoration. She came up with a plan for the next day at school and then she sincerely prayed to her Savior.
> C.W. Brush Prairie, WA
>
> .....

Question: What do you think is Satan's purpose behind these and other products? Answer: To recruit young people to join his rebellion against God.

Note: You may find the periodic newsletter "Plugged In" helpful as you guide your kids through the dangerous waters of media discernment. It is available from Focus on the Family at 1-800-232-6459 or www.family.org. (Ages 9–18)

Dinner Table Discussion
Is Satan Real? Many people have a hard time believing that there is a literal person called Satan who is behind the evil of our world. This is often because the image they have is of a cartoonish, horned character with a pitchfork, rather than an intelligent, seductive, deceptive personality with a vast network of demonic

servants. A good topic for a dinner table discussion is the nature and work of Satan. Unlike a dinner table debate, dinner table discussions seek to wrestle with the implications rather than argue the validity of an idea. The entire family can discuss whether Satan is an invention of superstition or a literal person. Does the Bible really present Satan as a fallen angel leading a rebellion against God? What view of Satan is most consistent with what we observe in the world around us? What difference does it make in how we live?

The best place to start gathering information for this discussion is with the passages listed earlier in this chapter. It is important to note that there is much debate on the topic of how and when Satan works today. We have found the following resources helpful in examining the topic, whether or not you fully agree with their emphasis.

The Bondage Breaker by Neil Anderson (Harvest House: 1990)
Victory Over the Darkness by Neil Anderson (Regal Books: 1990)
The Screwtape Letters by C.S. Lewis (various pubishers)
Behind the Glittering Mask by Mark Rutland (Vine Books: 1996)

Movie Night
Films which can be used to emphasize the reality and work of Satan include the following.

The Truman Show: In this film, the main character, Truman (played by Jim Carrey), is unaware that he is living on a giant television set and that his every action is being broadcast to the world. Every person in his life is an actor or actress, every scene a prop, every discussion a scripted set-up to see how he will respond. As the story unfolds, Truman begins to realize that there is something wrong with his world, and he seeks to discover whether or not there is a world beyond the one in which he is trapped. Another key character in the film is the producer/director of the *Truman*

Show. He calls himself "the creator . . . of a television show," and his task is to manipulate Truman's surroundings to make him think it is reality, when in fact it is all a grand deception. The film ends when Truman finally overcomes a long series of obstacles to discover the real world. After viewing this film, ask the following discussion questions.

Question: How is the producer/director like Satan? Answer: He manipulates and deceives Truman into believing what is not true.

Question: How are we like Truman? Answer: We sense that there is a reality beyond our experience, but we must overcome the obstacles of deception Satan throws our way.

Question: What passage of Scripture does this film illustrate? Answer: John 8:44, because it illustrates how Satan can manipulate our lives through deception and lies.

Question: What is the lesson for us? Answer: We must discern truth from lies in every aspect of life.

The Devil and Daniel Webster: This classic film portrays the Devil as one who gives us what we want in order to get what he wants. The Devil finds a poor, struggling farmer who is overwhelmed by the troubles of life. He sells his soul to the Devil in exchange for seven years of good fortune. After becoming a wealthy, influential man in the community, this farmer faces pay day and must give up everything. Enter Daniel Webster, who agrees to risk his own freedom in order to redeem the foolish victim of Satan's scheme. After viewing the film, ask the following discussion questions.

Question: How did the Devil get the man to sell his soul? Answer: By offering him a way out of his troubles, giving him seven years of good fortune.

Question: Did the Devil do this because he cared about the man? Answer: No. He did it in order to get what he wanted—the man's soul.

Question: What passages of Scripture does this film illustrate? Answer: 1 Peter 5:8, because the Devil is seeking someone to destroy, and 2 Corinthians 11:14, because the Devil masquerades as a good guy while trying to trap us.

Question: What is the lesson for us? Answer: Be aware that Satan will offer short-term gain in exchange for our long-term destruction.

Someone to Watch Over Me (Adventures in Odyssey animated video)—This story of a boy who falls into a coma after an accident portrays the reality of spiritual warfare through his encounters with danger and the protection of God's angel. (Ages 5–10)

Drive Time or Bedtime Audios

Several Adventures in Odyssey and other audio resources address the reality and work of Satan, including the following.

"Darkness Before Dawn" (AIO Album #25 or episodes #324–334)—These episodes deal with the reality of spiritual warfare. This series is not recommended for younger listeners. (Ages 10 and up)

"The Magician's Nephew" and "The Lion, the Witch and the Wardrobe"—This audio series' portrayal of the White Witch is a powerful analogy of Satan and his schemes. (Radio Theatre dramatization of C.S. Lewis' Chronicles of Narnia series is produced by and available from Focus on the Family.)

Chapter 7

What Is the Bible?

A little boy opened the big old family Bible. With fascination, he looked at each page as he turned it. Partway through Genesis, something fell out of the Bible to the floor. He picked it up and examined it closely. It was an old leaf from a tree that had been pressed in between the pages years earlier.

"Mommy, look what I found," the boy called out.

"What have you got there?" his mother asked.

With astonishment in the young boy's voice, he answered, "It's Adam's suit!"

Do you remember the days when it was common for a large family Bible to be displayed on the coffee table? A prized household possession, it weighed at least fifteen pounds, usually contained a record of key family names and events, and featured a gallery of classic paintings illustrating some of the "big" stories like Moses at the burning bush and David facing the giant Goliath. Often, you could find an occasional treasure from the past between its pages—such as old birth and baptism certificates, crayon drawings from childhood, or Adam's suit.

Once upon a time, whether it was used or not, the family

Bible was seen at the center of family conversation and life. Today, the *TV Guide* and remote control have displaced the large family Bible atop the coffee table. Where the Bible was once the central symbol of family guidance, cable and network programming now have taken its place.

The disappearance of the family Bible is symbolic of a lost understanding of the Scriptures. Many children have no idea what the Bible really is because their parents view it as an outdated relic too heavy to place at the center of family life. As a result, popular media and peers shape their values more than the revealed truth of God.

Even many Christian homes that routinely reference the Bible do so without truly understanding why. Why do we look to the Bible as our source of truth? Where did the Bible come from? Who wrote it? Why should we give it any more respect than other great works of history? These and other questions should be answered if we are to use the Bible as the basis of the beliefs and values we are teaching.

What to Understand

The third key component to a Christian worldview is understanding the importance of God's revelation to mankind—the Scriptures. In order to identify true north with regard to the Bible, the following should be understood.

> **Importance:** There are many ways people see the Bible. Some view it as a great work of literature, some consider it a historical chronicle of Jews and early Christians, while still others read it as God's supernatural revelation to mankind. In truth, the Bible is all these things and more. It is the compass pointing true north. It is the light of truth that dispels the darkness of deception. It is, quite simply, the Word of God. Therefore, we must help our children establish "normal" by teaching them the Christian view of the Scriptures.

Compass Belief: The Bible is God's written message to mankind. It tells us what we need to know about God, ourselves and the world in which we live. It points "true north" by lighting our path with truth.

Supporting Scriptures: The following passages describe key aspects of God's revealed truth through the Bible.

THE BIBLE IS FROM GOD

Above all, you must understand that no prophecy of Scripture came about by the prophet's own interpretation. For prophecy never had its origin in the will of man, but men spoke from God as they were carried along by the Holy Spirit (2 Peter 1:20-21).

All Scripture is God-breathed and is useful for teaching, rebuking, correcting and training in righteousness, so that the man of God may be thoroughly equipped for every good work (2 Timothy 3:16-17).

THE BIBLE IS TRUTH

For the word of the Lord is right and true; he is faithful in all he does (Psalm 33:4).

I tell you the truth, until heaven and earth disappear, not the smallest letter, not the least stroke of a pen, will by any means disappear from the Law until everything is accomplished (Matthew 5:18).

Sanctify them by the truth; your word is truth (John 17:17).

THE BIBLE IS OUR GUIDE

How can a young man keep his way pure? By living according to your word (Psalm 119:9).

Your word is a lamp to my feet and a light for my path (Psalm 119:105).

And we have the word of the prophets made more certain, and you will do well to pay attention to it, as to a light shining in a dark place, until the day dawns and the morning star rises in your hearts (2 Peter 1:19).

Impression Points

Following are several ideas for teaching the importance of the Bible to children of various ages. Pick and choose the impression points that will work best for your family.

Real Life Moments

When You Walk By the Way: The most natural way to teach our children the importance of the Bible is to incorporate it into the daily conversations we have with them. It isn't necessary to set aside a formal time of instruction and Bible study to apply Scripture to our lives. It is every bit as effective (perhaps more so) to refer to what the Bible says on a given topic as we discuss various issues over the dinner table, while taking a walk, or while correcting wrong behavior or rewarding right behavior.

When You Lie Down and Rise Up: More than ever before, the tools exist today to help our children begin the habit of regular Bible reading in the morning or evening. From products like *The Beginners Bible* for preschoolers, and the *New International Version Kid's Devotional Bible* for older elementary kids, to various teen devotional Bibles, there is a Bible resource right for your child whatever his or her age. A few minutes a day

> . . . . .
>
> ## Baking Bread
>
> Every Christmas our home is filled with the smell of pumpkin bread baking. We bake at least three dozen loaves to give to friends and family. From the time our son was four, he has been helping me bake the bread. It makes him feel that he is an important part of our family tradition.
>
> G.A. Blue Jay, CA
>
> . . . . .

with an age-appropriate Bible will begin your child on a lifelong journey of allowing God's Word to light the path of life.

On the Doorposts: We seem to have lost the significance of symbols in the home. A large family Bible once graced many a coffee table as a tangible reminder that we look beyond personal opinion for guidance. We look to the truth revealed in the pages of Scripture. Whether you use a large family Bible or Scripture quotations hanging on the walls, find ways to place symbols in your home which reflect the importance of the Bible in your family experience. Without saying a word, these symbols will quietly reinforce the fact that God has given us an objective guide to truth.

Planned Activities

Light to My Path: On a particularly dark evening, turn out every light in the house and enjoy a "light to my path" scavenger hunt with the kids. Create a list of things in the house that you need to find. Give each child a flashlight to light his path as he searches for the various objects on your list. Once the kids have success-fully gathered all of the required items, reward them with a bowl of ice cream while you read Psalm 119:105 and compare your adventure with the scavenger hunt to how the Bible lights our path of life. (Ages 4–9)

Following Directions: Tell your kids that you have planned an exciting outing to someplace special. You may or may not choose to reveal the destination, but make it a place you know they enjoy such as a favorite restaurant, ice-cream shop, mini-golf course, bowling alley, a movie theater, etc. Create a special map that has step-by-step directions to the location. Assign a child to help you navigate. As the child tells you which direc-tion to turn, ignore her instructions. Tell her that you know what you are doing and you don't need to heed the map. Your child will likely become very frustrated with you, insisting that you follow the directions so that you don't get lost. After several turns, stop the car and admit that you are lost. Give the kids a chance to scold you for failing to follow the map. Ask them what you should do next. They will say go back to the start and follow the directions. This time, do as they say. Upon arriving at the special location, read 2 Timothy 3:16-17 and/or Psalm 119:105 and share that God gave us the Bible as a life map, and that those who are wise obey its directions. (Ages 4–10)

Junior Detectives: Play a game of "Junior Detectives" by telling the kids you have several clues for them to find, all of which help answer the question "What is it?" They must become detectives in order to figure out what the "it" is. Here is your game plan.

Hide six items around the house that represent a characteristic of the Bible. We used the following items.

A Flashlight: It gives us light in the darkness.

A Ruler: It tells us if we are right or wrong.

An Encyclopedia: It tells us what is true.

An Adventures in Odyssey Audio Cassette: It tells us wonderful stories.

A Compass: It points the right way when we are lost.

A Cross: It tells us about Jesus.

Write clues for finding each item as well as the above fill-in statements on six pieces of paper and enclose them in six envelopes. For example, the first clue might read, "The first clue you will meet, by looking in Dad's favorite seat." Followed by, "It gives us _____ in the darkness."

Have fun with the kids going through each clue. Let the youngest to the oldest child try to answer the question "What is it?" after examining each clue.

Once someone has guessed that "it" is the Bible, read 2 Timothy 3:16-17 together and discuss all that the Bible is to our lives. (Ages 6–10)

Personal Stories

Date Discussion: Get into the habit of taking your children on dates such as periodic breakfast outings with just Mom or just Dad. Use the opportunities to tell them personal stories from your life. On each date, tell your child how the Bible has impacted your life. We all have such experiences, but rarely think to share them with our children. Take a few minutes to reflect upon passages of Scripture that have meant a great deal to you, then share them with your kids. Our children need to hear more than theory and principles; they need to know that the beliefs you're passing on to them have had a real impact in your life. You don't need to be profound, just real. Here are a few examples that may help your creative thinking.

"While in college, I was reading James 1:5 which says to ask for wisdom if you lack it—so I did. I asked God for the wisdom that He promised to give to those who ask. Do you know what happened next? I didn't suddenly gain instant brilliance. I was given a deep and passionate desire to learn. Over time, this drive to learn caused me to gain insights and experience in areas I never imagined myself having any 'wisdom.' This experience taught me that God will fulfill the promises of His Word, but not always in the way we might expect."

"During a particularly difficult time in my life, I found myself drawn to the Book of Job. Job is the story of how a good man endured great difficulty, never knowing why it was happening. His friends told him that bad things were happening because he must have sinned. In the end, he discovered that he had done nothing wrong—and that bad things were happening for reasons beyond his understanding. I realized then that, regardless of what happens, God is in control, and I can trust Him even if I don't understand what is going on."

Identify those moments in your life when the Bible played an important role and tell them to your children.

Entertainment
Last Chance Detectives: There are three videos in this live-action series from Focus on the Family for kids ages 8–13. Each episode is built around two symbols—a pocket compass and a Bible—both showing that there is truth beyond our experience that can guide our way.

The Storykeepers: This animated video series for ages 6–12 helps children appreciate the risks taken by the early church in order to read and preserve the Bible. A group of believers in Rome hold secret meetings in order to tell the stories of Jesus. They are under constant threat of arrest and persecution.

Drive Time or Bedtime Audios
Adventures in Odyssey: Several episodes of this radio drama series, available from Focus on the Family, reinforce the authority and significance of the Bible in our lives. Specific titles to look for include the following.
   "Hidden in My Heart" (AIO episode #321)
   "A Worker Approved" (AIO episode #59)
   "The Case of the Delinquent Disciples" (AIO episode #249)

The Singing Bible: This set of audio tapes presents the entire Bible through song and dialogue in a fun and memorable manner. Ideal for younger kids (4–7), this series gives children an overview of the entire Bible in a few hours. Great for bedtime and drive-time listening!

Musicals: There are many wonderful children's church musicals produced each year that have tapes available. Check with your local Christian store and ask for a catalog of children's musicals that tell various Bible stories.

Movie Night
Films that can be used to emphasize the significance of the Bible include the following.

The Turner Bible Collection: This series accurately drama-tizes several Bible stories including Abraham, Joseph, Moses, and others.

The Ten Commandments: No child should grow up with-out seeing Charlton Heston playing the part of Moses at least once!

The Prince Of Egypt: This powerful animated film is a wonderful retelling of the Exodus story and captures the majesty of God's work using state of the art technology and imagination.

Dinner Table Debate

Is the Bible Trustworthy? Set a dinner table debate around the theme of whether or not the Bible is reliable. Many claim that the Bible is filled with errors and cannot be trusted. Others say it is only reliable when it speaks to spiritual issues but not histori-cal and factual issues. Still others claim that it is the infallible and authoritative Word of God. Which is true? Divide into teams and plan for this important debate. Several resources to help as you prepare include the following.

Know What You Believe by Paul Little—A popular, introduc-tory level book to systematic theology. Covers such topics as the Bible, God, Jesus Christ, man and sin, etc.

Know Why You Believe by Paul Little—A popular, introduc-tory level text on apologetics. Covers such questions as "Is Christianity rational?" "Did Christ rise from the dead?" etc.

Why Believe the Bible by John MacArthur.

→ Chapter 8 ←

Who Am I?

⚬⚬⚬

"Mom, where did I come from?" asked six-year-old Bobby.

He had overheard some older kids on the playground discussing the subject, awakening his curiosity. Unsure how best to respond, his mother thought for a moment. She had not planned to discuss the birds and bees while her son was so young. But, having no idea what kinds of things the older kids might have put into his head, she couldn't very well avoid the topic now. Hence, she took a deep breath, drew all her wits about her, and proceeded with the explanation.

After several minutes listening to Mom describe things like the love between a man and wife and a detailed description of the reproductive process, Bobby was sorry he asked.

Puzzled by his response, Mom asked Bobby if he had any questions about what she had explained.

"Not really. You see, Paul said he came from Chicago, and Lisa said she came from Florida. So I was wondering where I came from."

One of the most basic questions deep within the human

spirit is, "Who am I?" We all want to know where we came from, why we are here, and whether there is a purpose to our lives. How we answer this question for our children will shape their perception of life in so many ways.

In an essay written in 1946, C.S. Lewis spoke of how the two dominant perspectives of life will impact the way we live.

> *The one believes that men are going to live forever, that they were created by God and so built that they can find their true and lasting happiness only by being united to God, that they have gone badly off the rails, and that obedient faith in Christ is the only way back. The other believes that men are an accidental result of the blind workings of matter, that they started as mere animals and have more or less steadily improved, that they are going to live for about seventy years, that their happiness is fully attainable by good social services and political organizations, and that everything else is to be judged to be "good" or "bad" simply insofar as it helps or hinders that kind of "happiness."* [1]

Our generation is facing a crisis of meaning. We have lost sight of the purpose and identity that come from understanding the truth about ourselves. In this context, we must help our children develop a biblical perspective of themselves.

What to Understand

The fourth key component to a Christian worldview is understanding how we human beings fit into the grand picture. In order to identify true north with regard to our purpose and nature, the following should be understood.

Importance: The deepest yearning within mankind is to understand who we are and why we are here. Sadly, many have no answers to these questions, and are robbed of any sense of purpose or meaning. Others have false answers, which causes them to live a life out of step with reality. It is vital that we give our children a sense of "normal" by teaching them who they are, why they are here, and why they are as they are.

Compass Belief: We are spiritual beings created for the purpose of relationship with God. Because we are made in God's image, we have tremendous capacity for good. Due to the disease called sin, we tend toward evil. We have a free will and are accountable to God for our choices.

Supporting Scriptures: The following passages describe key aspects of the nature of man.

WE ARE SPIRITUAL BEINGS IN GOD'S IMAGE

So God created man in his own image, in the image of God he created him; male and female he created them (Genesis 1:27).
And the dust returns to the ground it came from, and the spirit returns to God who gave it (Ecclesiastes 12:7).
What is man that you are mindful of him, the son of man that you care for him? You made him a little lower than the heavenly beings and crowned him with glory and honor (Psalm 8:4-5).

WE HAVE CAPACITY FOR GOOD

The Lord said, . . . "Nothing they plan to do will be impossible for them" (Genesis 11:6).
Here is the conclusion of the matter: Fear God and keep his commandments, for this is the whole duty of man (Ecclesiastes 12:13).
Consecrate yourselves and be holy, because I am holy (Leviticus 11:44).

WE TEND TOWARD EVIL

For all have sinned and fall short of the glory of God (Romans 3:23).
Therefore, just as sin entered the world through one man, and death through sin, and in this way death came to all men,

because all sinned. . . . Through the disobedience of the one man the many were made sinners (Romans 5:12, 19).
But each one is tempted when, by his own evil desire, he is dragged away and enticed. Then, after desire has conceived, it gives birth to sin; and sin, when it is full-grown, gives birth to death (James 1:14-15).
For the wages of sin is death (Romans 6:23).

WE ARE ACCOUNTABLE FOR CHOOSING
Love the Lord your God with all your heart (Mark 12:30).
For God will bring every deed into judgment, including every hidden thing, whether it is good or evil (Ecclesiastes 12:14).
Do not be deceived: God cannot be mocked. A man reaps what he sows. The one who sows to please his sinful nature, from that nature will reap destruction; the one who sows to please the Spirit, from the Spirit will reap eternal life (Galatians 6:7-8).

Impression Points
Following are several ideas for teaching the nature of man to children of various ages. Pick and choose the impression points that will work best for your family.

Real Life Moments
Celebrating Creativity: There are literally hundreds of opportunities during a year to emphasize with our children that we are creative because we are made in the image of a creative God. Every day your children do something creative, giving you a chance to emphasize this wonderful truth. Whether baking cookies together, hanging that special drawing on the refrigerator, or examining a newly engineered Lego building, capture these special moments to celebrate the creative capacity we received from God. It is as simple as saying "You are so creative! Just like God."

Identifying Sin: Just as children provide hundreds of opportunities each year to point out their wonderful creative capacity, they also give us ample opportunity to point out the negative. Children sin, just as their parents do. As parents, it is our job to equip our children to understand and counter the evil within them. We cannot assume them innocent, when history and Scripture tell us that they are prone to evil. We owe it to them to understand the source and nature of the evil within the human heart—namely, sin. Though unpleasant, we must intentionally link wrong behavior to the reality of sin.

Mountain Top Experience

We have a great love for the outdoors through camping, snow skiing, and hiking. We sit on a mountaintop and share the fact that God created all this for us to enjoy.
L.K. Clovis, CA

When our children reach age four or five, we need to go beyond merely correcting wrong behavior. We need to begin explaining the nature and consequence of sin. It is not necessary to be heavy-handed or condemning. But when they are feeling remorse, we need to call sin by its name. Simple comments such as, "When you got angry and pushed that boy, that was a sin," or, "When you stole that piece of candy, that was a sin," help to connect wrong behavior to the reality of sin. Of course, you should also capture the opportunity to invite the child to pray, asking God to forgive the sin committed. In this way, we begin to establish an understanding that we do sin, that it must be dealt with, and, most importantly, that God is always ready to forgive our sins.

In the Same Boat: To avoid giving the impression to your children that they are sinful but you are not, make sure to admit that you are in the same boat. Without going into too much detail, tell your kids that you sin too. You may want to tell them about

times in your life when you did something sinful, and the consequences of that action. Also, when you say something you
shouldn't because you are in a bad mood, don't excuse it away—
confess it as wrong, as sin. When you lose your temper with the
kids over a minor irritation, swallow your pride long enough to
admit you were wrong, and that you too need to confess your
sin and be accountable before God for your actions and choices.

Planned Activities
Spittin' Image: A fun activity that illustrates being made in God's
image is to trace the outline of each child's body onto a very
large piece of paper (or smaller pieces taped together). Once the
outline is traced, have your child color in the features: face,
clothes, etc. in order to make the drawing into the "spittin'
image" of herself. As your children color their drawings, read
Genesis 1:24-27 and discuss some of the ways, such as the following, we are in God's image.

God is love, so we can love.

God makes choices, so we make choices.

God feels happy and sad, so we feel happy and sad.

God hears, so we have ears.

God sees, so we have eyes.

(Ages 4–8) (*Family Night Tool Chest: Basic Christian Beliefs* p. 23)

> *Play-Doh People:* A variation on the same concept for
> younger children is to get out some Play-Doh and make lit-
> tle people. Tell the kids that each of us is going to make a
> little person in our own image, once again discussing the
> ways in which we are created in God's image. (*Family
> Night Tool Chest: Basic Christian Beliefs* p. 24)

> *Blinded by Sin:* In order to illustrate the difference between
> the "disease" of sin and sinful acts, create a walking path obsta-
> cle course somewhere in the house using toys, shoes, pillows,

balloons, or anything you wish for the kids to maneuver around. Have a contest to see who can walk through the obstacle course the fastest without touching any of the items on the path. Add to the fun by ringing a bell or yelling "Sin!" whenever someone touches one of the objects. Next, take turns trying to do the same course while blindfolded. The bell will be ringing like mad as the disease of sin (represented by the blindfold) affects each person's ability to avoid sinning (represented by touching the items). Relate this activity to the message of Romans 5:12, 19, which describes the fact that we all have a sinful nature. (Ages 5–10)

Entertainment
Movie Night: Films that can be used to emphasize the dual nature of man and the fact that we are accountable for our choices include the following.

A Christmas Carol: There are various versions of this wonderful classic to be enjoyed each Christmas season. But there is more message in this story than we often realize. It is not just about a guy who didn't like Christmas. It is a tale of repentance and redemption. Ebenezer Scrooge is a powerful symbol of the choice each of us must make in life—either to follow our selfish, sinful nature or submit to God and reflect His image in our attitudes and actions. If you wish to use a radio drama rather than film version of this story, the Focus on the Family Radio Theatre adaptation is excellent. And one particularly child friendly movie version which follows the book very closely is *The Muppet's Christmas Carol.* Here are a few discussion questions to use as you reflect upon the film.

Question: Was Scrooge made in the image of God? Answer: Yes, but he certainly didn't live like it!

Question: In what ways did Scrooge show he had a sinful heart? Answer: He was selfish, stingy, mean, etc., all of which show the dark side of people.

Question: After he realized he was wrong, what did Scrooge do? Answer: He turned away from the wrong toward the right. He repented and showed it by changing his ways!

Lord of the Flies: In this disturbing yet profound story, a group of well-educated, well-behaved English boys find themselves stranded on a deserted island after a plane crash. With no adults to take charge, the boys must establish a system of order to work together toward survival. As the story unfolds, these mannerly children become ill-disciplined, self-subverting animals. Ralph, the kind, natural leader, is rejected and attacked. The chubby outsider (Piggy) fears for and eventually loses his life. The group of well-behaved children turns into savages. They subvert order, embrace cruelty, and kill the weak. If not for the timely intervention of a rescue team, they would have continued toward eventual self-destruction. This classic story is available on film. The message at its core is one of evil in our world—and more troubling—in our hearts. Here are a few questions to draw out the key lessons of the film.

Question: Were these boys good or bad at the beginning of the story? Answer: They were both, but basically good.

Question: Why did some of them become so cruel and evil later in the story? Answer: Because there were no adults to keep them from doing bad.

Question: Did the evil come from outside or inside these boys? Answer: From within their hearts.

Question: What Bible verse does this movie illustrate? Answer: James 1:14-15.

Chapter 9

Why Believe in Jesus?

Six-year-old Brianna has been helping her father conduct the evening's family night activity. They have been discussing what it means to have Jesus living in our hearts. Having just recently grasped the concept herself, she thought it would be a good idea to share this important truth with two-year-old brother Nathan.

"Jesus died for our sins, Nathan. And He wants to come live in our hearts and clean out the sin and bring us to heaven after we die." So far, so good. Nathan is still with her. Then comes the big question. "Nathan, would you like to ask Jesus to come live in your heart?"

At two, Nathan doesn't want anyone crawling inside his heart, so he responds with an indignant "No!"

Oh well, perhaps another day.

There are some concepts that are more difficult than others to explain to children. But none is more important than introducing them to and inviting them into relationship with Jesus Christ. The Christian faith is built upon understanding who Jesus is, what He did, and why He did it.

What to Understand

The fifth key component to a Christian worldview is understanding the person and work of Jesus Christ. In order to identify true north with regard to Jesus, the following should be understood.

Importance: There are many views regarding who Jesus Christ was and is. Our children will encounter those who consider Jesus a great moral teacher, an important prophet, or a mere legend. It is our job as Christian parents to teach them the truth—that Jesus Christ is the Son of God who died for our sins and rose from the dead to conquer death.

Compass Belief: Jesus Christ is God. He came in human form, lived a perfect life, and gave His life as payment for our sins. He defeated death by rising from the dead and is preparing a place in heaven for all who accept the gift of salvation He has provided.

Supporting Scriptures: The following passages describe key aspects of who Jesus is and why He came.

JESUS IS THE SON OF GOD

The Word became flesh and made his dwelling among us. We have seen his glory, the glory of the One and Only, who came from the Father, full of grace and truth (John 1:14).

"I tell you the truth," Jesus answered, "before Abraham was born, I am" (John 8:58).

"But what about you?" he asked. "Who do you say I am?" Simon Peter answered, "You are the Christ, the Son of the living God." Jesus replied, "Blessed are you, Simon son of Jonah, for this was not revealed to you by man, but by my Father in heaven" (Matthew 16:15-16).

JESUS DIED TO PAY THE PENALTY FOR OUR SINS

The next day John saw Jesus coming toward him and said, "Look, the Lamb of God, who takes away the sin of the world" (John 1:29).

*"For God so loved the world that he gave his one and only
Son, that whoever believes in him shall not perish but have
eternal life"* (John 3:16).
*For the wages of sin is death, but the gift of God is eternal life
in Christ Jesus our Lord* (Romans 6:23).

JESUS IS THE ONLY WAY

*Jesus answered, "I am the way and the truth and the life. No
one comes to the Father except through me"* (John 14:6).
*"For God did not send his Son into the world to condemn the
world, but to save the world through him. Whoever believes
in him is not condemned, but whoever does not believe stands
condemned already because he has not believed in the name of
God's one and only Son"* (John 3:17-18).
*For it is by grace you have been saved, through faith—and
this is not from yourselves, it is the gift of God—not by
works, so that no one can boast* (Ephesians 2:8-9).

Impression Points _____

Following are several ideas for teaching about Jesus Christ to
children of various ages. Pick and choose the impression points
that will work best for your family.

Real Life Moments

Church Attendance: It is easy to overlook the importance of
attending church services every weekend with our children.
Making church attendance a natural, normal part of our lives
makes a significant statement to our children. When they see
that Mom and Dad consider worshiping the Lord a central part
of life—even though it would be more relaxing to stay home
and read the paper—it communicates a level of commitment
and submission to Christ few people demonstrate in this day. So
find a solid, Bible-teaching church that emphasizes the lordship
of Jesus Christ and attend regularly. Although many churches

separate the family every week into adult and kids' church services, it is nice when the kids are old enough to sit through the service so that you are all hearing the same thing at the same time, allowing for discussion later. You may also consider helping teach or assist in the Sunday School program so that you can hear the same things your kids are hearing, again allowing for more meaningful discussion later.

Other Beliefs: The central truth of the Christian faith is that Jesus Christ is God. So how do we respond when our children develop relationships with those who do not believe as we do about Jesus? He claimed to be the only way to God (John 14:6). But our kids will have relationship with schoolteachers, neighbors, even those within our own immediate or extended families who reject the claims of Christ. There are nice, sincere people who seem moral and religious, but who do not embrace the fundamental teaching of our faith. How we respond in such situations will make a significant statement to our children about how seriously we take the claims of Christ. In John 3:18 Jesus said, "Whoever does not believe stands condemned already because he has not believed in the name of God's one and only Son." As hard as this truth may be, it is important that we avoid the temptation to suggest that other beliefs are equally valid. Certainly, we need to be loving, charitable, and kind to people with different beliefs. But the hard reality is that Jesus did not allow room for us to include Him in with a

> . . . . .
>
> ## Music Time
>
> For Christmas, we gave each of our sons a guitar. For twenty minutes before bedtime the boys and I practice the guitar together. Although we are all learning how to play, we are focused on enjoying each other and the "music" together.
>
> *S.S. Englewood, CO*
>
> . . . . .

smorgasbord of other religious ideas. He is either God or He isn't. Ours is a very exclusive faith, in that Jesus Christ claimed to be the only way (John 14:6). It is also a very inclusive faith, in that He said anyone and everyone are welcome (John 3:16).

Because several members of our extended family reject Jesus Christ as Lord, we have found it necessary to handle some tough discussions with our kids. For example, being aware that a certain family member does not believe in Jesus, our six year old recently asked whether or not that person will go to heaven. Here are some suggestions on handling these sometimes awkward moments.

What to Say. . .

"Not everyone believes in Jesus yet. We need to love them and show them Jesus in our lives."

"We don't know for certain what he/she believes in his/her heart. We should just pray that he/she will understand and believe in Jesus if he/she doesn't already."

"Jesus said that not everyone will accept His love."

"It makes us sad that (name) rejects Jesus, but we will continue to love him/her like God does and pray that someday he/she will believe."

What Not to Say . . .

"They are evil people who will burn in hell for eternity!"

"Not everyone believes in Jesus, but they are good so I'm sure God will accept them anyway."

"Let's not talk about that."

Again, these are difficult discussions, but we must tell the truth while modeling a sensitive and loving spirit toward those who do not accept Jesus Christ.

Leading Your Child into the Kingdom: On page 198 of this book is a summary of the steps involved in leading your child to Christ when he or she is ready. This is nothing that can be scheduled or forced, but something we should be prepared to handle when our children have reached a point of understanding and readiness. Remember that we are not the only ones working on the spiritual development of our children. God Himself is working within the hearts of each of your children. And when He is drawing them near, we need to be ready to walk our children through the wonder of spiritual birth!

Sign on the Dotted Line: Stan and his son Eddie are pals. But they also have a binding contract relationship with one another. When his son turned eight years old, Stan drafted a contract with his son that still hangs signed on the wall today—a reminder of their mutual agreement. It reads like this . . .

> We, the undersigned, on this 25th day of December 1991, do hereby agree to live our lives in obedience to God's Word, The Bible, and to keep Jesus Christ as the Lord of our lives.
>
> In doing so, "Party A" gives assurance to "Party B" that he (she) will be in heaven, so as to have an eternity to spend together. As did "Party A," "Party B" gives assurance to "Party A" that he (she) will be in heaven, making the eternal relationship possible.
>
> Both parties recognize that entrance into heaven is not the result of their works, but rather by the Grace of God, through the death of Jesus Christ on the Cross. We also hereby ask the Holy Spirit for His help in meeting the terms of this contract.
>
> It is this saving work of the Lord Jesus Christ that gives the undersigned the confidence to enter into this agreement. With men, it would be impossible, but with God, All Things Are Possible!
>
> Signed This Day, Before Jehovah God:
>
> _____   _____
> Stanley R. John (aka: Daddy)   Date
>
> _____   _____
> Eddie John (aka: Son)   Date

Eddie will never forget the importance of his decision to follow Christ thanks to Dad's effort to create this wonderful impression point.

Planned Activities
Christmas and Easter: The Christmas and Easter seasons provide a very natural, annual opportunity for emphasizing the work and person of Jesus Christ. Sadly, we often become so busy and consumed by the fun traditions of these holidays (Santa Claus, tree decorating, turkey or ham dinners, Easter egg hunts) that we miss reflecting upon and celebrating the reason for these seasons—Jesus Christ. Look for ways to emphasize Jesus Christ amid the celebration of Christmas and Easter in your home. Here are a few ideas for the creatively challenged.

Christmas Advent Calendar: There are several Advent calendars on the market each Christmas season. Some are nothing more than pictures with a candy for each day. Fun for the kids, but hardly useful in teaching our children about the coming of Jesus Christ. Try to find an Advent calendar that tells a small part of the Christmas story each day. They are more expensive, but worth the investment. Another option for those who are more creative is to design and create your own. Using this simple tool each Christmas season will help you capture the opportunity to talk with your kids about who Jesus is and why He came.

Christmas Advent Candle/Wreath: A fun family activity during the Christmas season is to buy materials from a craft store and work together to create an Advent wreath. Include five candles—four on the outer ring and one in the center. One evening each week for the four weeks leading up to Christmas, light a candle together while reading or reciting the words of Matthew 1:23 saying that Jesus would be called "Immanuel, God with us." On Christmas Eve or day, light the center, final candle and read the entire

Christmas story found in Luke 2. In this simple way, you capture the opportunity to emphasize the reality of the Incarnation—that God became man. (Ages 5–12)

Christmas Lights Outing: When you take a drive to see Christmas lights in your town next Christmas, use the opportunity to explain to your children that hanging Christmas lights is a way we symbolize that Jesus is the light of the world as described in John 1:1-9 and John 8:12. In this and other ways, you can take advantage of the activities already on the holiday calendar to teach your children why to believe in Jesus. (Aes 5–10)

Easter Resurrection Eggs: One of the best ways to merge a traditional fun activity with the goal of teaching our children about Jesus is to incorporate "Resurrection Eggs" into your egg hunting plans. Number a dozen plastic eggs (the kind that open for placing candy or other items inside) one to twelve, and place the items listed below inside. Hide the eggs along with the candy or real eggs and begin the search. Once all the eggs have been found, have the children open each Resurrection Egg in order and recount the story of Christ's death, burial, and resurrection. You can make this part of your egg hunt extra exciting and special by giving a prize to the child who either finds the most resurrection eggs, or who finds the empty tomb egg. (Note: A pre-made set of Resurrection Eggs is available from FamilyLife Ministries for those who would rather purchase than create their own set. Call 800-FLTODAY [800-358-6329] for ordering information.)

Egg #1: A small cup and cracker (Symbol of Last Supper described in Matthew 26:26-28)

Egg #2: Three coins wrapped in foil (Symbol of betrayal by Judas described in Matthew 26:14-15)

Egg #3: A small whip made of a toothpick with string or rubber band strips (Symbol of flogging described in Mark 15:15)

Egg #4: A tiny robe pattern cut from purple cloth (Symbol of robe described in Mark 15:17)

Egg #5: A thorn (Symbol of crown of thorns described in Mark 15:17)

Egg #6: A cross (Symbol of cross described in John 19:17)

Egg #7: A scroll with "King of the Jews" written on it (Symbol of scroll described in Matthew 27:37)

Egg #8: A nail (Symbol of nailing hands to cross described in John 20:25)

Egg #9: A piece of sponge (Symbol of vinegar given to Jesus described in John 19:29-30)

Egg #10: A spear made of toothpicks (Symbol of spear used to pierce Jesus' side described in John 19:34)

Egg #11: A small rock (Symbol of stone used to cover the tomb as described in Luke 24:2)

Egg #12: Empty! (Symbol of empty tomb after resurrection described in Luke 24:6) (Ages 5–10)

Only One Way: This simple activity illustrates the fact that Jesus is the only way to God. Have the kids attempt to role a marble into a small jar or drinking glass from the top of a large piece of poster board. The board must remain straight during these first attempts. As they will discover, it is almost impossible to get the marble into the narrow head of the jar or glass. Next, turn the poster board over to discover a line drawn down the middle of the poster board with the name "Jesus Christ" written over the line. Help the children fold the poster board along the line, and then invite them to try rolling the marble into the jar or glass. Using the ravine created by the fold, it will be much easier to succeed. Read Matthew 7:13-14 and John 14:6 and discuss Jesus' claim to be the only way to God. You may wish to recite a short jingle to help your kids remember the principle: "Try as we may, there's only one way!" (Ages 6–10)

Dinner Table Debate

Who Was Jesus? Our children will encounter various views of Jesus as they mature, and we should prepare them to evaluate each. Schedule a dinner table debate assigning one team the position that Jesus is God, and the other that He was a good teacher, a moral example, a prophet, or just a legend who never did or said the things recorded in the Bible. Several helpful resources to prepare for this debate include the following:

More Than a Carpenter by Josh McDowell

Jesus Under Fire, General Editors Michael Wilkins and J.P. Moreland

Know What You Believe by Paul Little—A popular, introductory level book on systematic theology. Covers such topics as the Bible, God, Jesus Christ, man and sin, etc.

Know Why You Believe by Paul Little—A popular, introductory level text on apologetics. Covers such questions as "Is Christianity rational?" "Did Christ rise from the dead?" etc.

Entertainment

The Visual Bible: One of the best representations of the biblical Jesus is in the set of videos on the book of Matthew called *The Visual Bible.* A word-for-word reading and dramatization of Mathew's Gospel, this set is well worth the investment and something your family will enjoy watching time and time again. You can obtain a set at your local Christian store or by contacting the producers on the web at www.visualbible.com.

The Easter Storykeepers: This full-length animated feature tells the story of Jesus through the eyes of his persecuted followers in Rome. Ideal for ages 6–12.

Movie Night

Several films that present a biblical view of Jesus Christ include the following:

Ben Hur: This classic film, staring Charlton Heston as Judah Ben Hur, is based upon the novel by Lew Wallace. (Incidentally, Lew Wallace became a Christian through the writing of Ben Hur.) The life of Ben Hur reaches a crisis when he is confronted with the person and healing power of Jesus Christ. This film can stand on its own, but you may enjoy posing the following questions as you watch.

Question: Name four different times when Judah Ben Hur encountered Jesus. Answers: 1. When Jesus gave Judah water. 2. When Jesus was teaching on the hillside. 3. When Jesus was carrying His cross. 4. When the blood of Jesus healed his mother and sister.

Question: After Mesalla condemned Judah and his family, what was the primary emotion that motivated Judah? Answer: Hatred.

Question: In the end, what impact did Jesus have in the life of Judah Ben Hur? Answer: He showed that love and forgiveness are more powerful than hatred and revenge.

Jesus of Nazareth: One of the best films ever produced showing the life and work of Jesus Christ, including His death and resurrection. This film can stand on its own as great entertainment and reinforcement of the person of Jesus.

Drive Time or Bedtime Audios
Several Adventures in Odyssey and other audio resources address the person and work of Jesus Christ.

"Back to Bethlehem" (AIO episodes #135–137)

"The Star" (AIO episodes #176–177)

"Unto Us a Child Is Born" (AIO episode #294)

PART 3

Compass Values

→ Chapter 10 ←

Personal Worth

∽∾

The woman didn't fit in. Walking through the exclusive department store, her tattered clothes and unkempt hair made it clear she was from a less privileged class. Perhaps she stepped inside to warm up on the way to the homeless shelter downtown. She wandered from one display to another with no apparent destination. Some customers were starting to squirm, concerned she might create an unpleasant scene by blurting out an obscenity or asking for money.

As she approached the display featuring fancy party dresses, the woman stopped to stare in admiration. She had never seen such elegance. She could eat for a month with the money it would take to purchase just one. Catching a glimpse of herself in the mirror, she was reminded that she didn't belong in this world. Noticing the disdainful looks of others, she began to walk away, hoping to retreat to the world of outcasts from which she had come.

"May I help you, Madam?" came the seemingly sincere question.

"Oh, well, no. I was just leaving."

"I noticed you admiring these dresses. Would you like to try a few of them on?"

"Oh, I couldn't. But thank you. I'll just be leaving now."

"Sure you could. I think this one would highlight your beautiful eyes."

"Thank you, but I can't afford . . ."

"What's the harm in just trying them on to see how you look? I'll select a few more that fit your color scheme and unlock a dressing room for you."

For the next hour, the clerk brought one outfit after another to the woman, fully aware that her efforts would yield no commission.

The disheveled woman felt like a queen. She hadn't been treated with such dignity and respect for longer than she could remember.

As the woman left, her head was a bit higher than it had been when she had wandered into the store. That momentary escape from the sense of shame and embarrassment that had dominated her existence was worth more than she could express.

The sales clerk returned to her duties, feeling good about following company policy. "Treat every customer as if she is worth a million dollars!" Little did she know that another customer, one who was worth a million dollars, was watching the entire affair. The customer decided that day that she would do all of her shopping in that store, with the help of that sales clerk.

How we treat others is a direct reflection of how we view them. If we place people on a hierarchy of value, we will treat some well, others badly. If we view all people as having worth and dignity, we will treat all people with a level of respect. Our role as parents is to help our children understand the importance of following God's "company policy" of treating all people "as if they are worth a million dollars!"

What to Understand

Our first compass value provides a foundation for the others—understanding the basis of personal dignity and respect. In order to identify true north with regard to individual worth, the following should be understood.

> **Importance:** We live in a society that has lost any basis for human worth. When our culture embraced the view that man is the beginning and end of all things (humanism), it abandoned the foundation of human dignity. Efforts to affirm self-respect apart from God fail because they have no ultimate foundation. The result is always an externally imposed standard of performance, appearance, ability, or intelligence. By definition, this standard will include some and exclude others—creating a society of individuals chasing an illusive prize. Therefore, we must help our children escape the "rat race" of performance driven self-worth by instilling in them a sense of worth which comes from being made in the image of God Himself.

> **Compass Value:** We have self-worth and dignity because we are made in the image of God. It doesn't matter how we look, how smart we are, or what we can and can't do. We are valuable because God made us so. So we treat others with respect because of who they are, not what they've done.

Supporting Scriptures: The following passages establish the biblical perspective on human dignity and worth.

WE ARE MADE IN GOD'S IMAGE

So God created man in his own image, in the image of God he created him; male and female he created them (Genesis 1:27). What is man that you are mindful of him, the son of man that you care for him? You made him a little lower than the heavenly beings and crowned him with glory and honor (Psalm 8:4-5).

APPEARANCE, INTELLIGENCE, AND ABILITY DON'T MATTER

"Before I formed you in the womb I knew you, before you

were born I set you apart" (Jeremiah 1:5). (Note: We have worth as a person before we are even born!)

Then Peter began to speak: "I now realize how true it is that God does not show favoritism but accepts all men from every nation who fear him and do what is right" (Acts 10:34). (Note: All people are equally welcome to God.)

Religion that God our Father accepts as pure and faultless is this: to look after orphans and widows in their distress (James 1:27). (Note: Even those who can't care for themselves are worthy.)

WE ARE VALUABLE BECAUSE GOD MADE US

For you created my inmost being; you knit me together in my mother's womb. I praise you because I am fearfully and wonderfully made; your works are wonderful, I know that full well. My frame was not hidden from you when I was made in the secret place. When I was woven together in the depths of the earth, your eyes saw my unformed body. All the days ordained for me were written in your book before one of them came to be (Psalm 139:13-16).

TREAT OTHERS IN A RESPECTFUL MANNER

Show proper respect to everyone (1 Peter 2:17).

For God said, "Honor your father and mother" (Matthew 15:4).

Do not rebuke an older man harshly, but exhort him as if he were your father. Treat younger men as brothers, older women as mothers, and younger women as sisters, with absolute purity (1 Timothy 5:1-2).

RESPECT IS GIVEN, NOT EARNED

He who despises his neighbor sins, but blessed is he who is kind to the needy (Proverbs 14:21).

Slaves, submit yourselves to your masters with all respect, not only those who are good and considerate, but also to those who are harsh (1 Peter 2:18).

Give everyone what you owe him: If you owe taxes, pay taxes;
if revenue, then revenue; if respect, then respect; if honor,
then honor (Romans 13:7). (Note: This was said to the
Roman Christians living under the harsh reign of Nero,
certainly not one who had "earned" respect.)

Impression Points _____

Following are several ideas for instilling dignity and respect in
children of various ages. Pick and choose the impression points
that will work best for your family.

Real Life Moments

Affirming Moments: "I can't do it!" exclaimed our six-year-old
son, Shaun. Frustrated by his inability to read as well as his
eight-year-old brother, Kyle, he decided to throw in the towel
and give up trying to read the words on the page before him.
"I'm not very smart!"

Ever since he was a toddler, Shaun has been comparing himself to his older brother. Kyle could always run faster, jump farther,
play harder, and yes, read better. Stumbling over new three-letter
words in his early reader book has made the disparity all too obvious. "Why try?" Shaun wonders. He feels it would be better to
give up altogether—resigning to inadequacy.

"You are too smart!" I (Olivia) respond, trying to bolster
Shaun's waning self-confidence and thwart his effort to get out
of homework. "Don't worry about Kyle. He is much older and
has had more time to learn than you have. You just need to do
your best, and your best is great!"

Defeated frown turning to confident grin, Shaun proceeds to
conquer those three-letter words and complete the page.
Success!

When our children face those times when life tells them,
"You are worthless unless you possess intelligence, ability, or

beauty," ours is an important job. We must take the opportunity to praise and affirm them as they are. In so doing, we model the attitude of a God who loves and accepts us based upon who we are, not what we do or how we appear!

The Wonder of Life: One of the most exciting seasons of family life is when Mom is expecting another baby. Kids of all ages become excited about the little child growing inside Mommy's tummy. This is a perfect time to share the wonder and security of God's design. Some of the moments to share with your children during pregnancy include the following.

Feeling the baby kick. Describe his or her attitudes, desires, etc., to begin affirming the humanness of this unborn baby. Say, "I guess he is feeling a bit cramped in there!" or "He is mad right now" or "I think she hears you singing to her!"

> .....
>
> *Christmastime*
>
> During the month of December, we take one night a week and drive to various parts of town and look at the Christmas lights. Dad always makes this a fun time by singing his nutty renditions of Christmas songs. We also talk about the meaning of Christmas and the different symbols like the tree, the star, and the lights.
>
> *S.K. Clovis, CA*
>
> .....

Taking the kids with you to the doctor appointment to hear the baby's heartbeat or to see the sonogram. Share the wonder of God weaving this little child in His own image.

Anticipating how life will be different with a new little sibling. Emphasize how much you already love this gift from God, not because of what he or she does, but because the baby is part of your family.

Giving Respect: Make a hard and fast rule in your home—

"There is never an excuse for treating others with disrespect!" Demand that everyone in the family (including Mom and Dad) treats others with respect. No demeaning, ignoring, or making others feel unimportant. When Mom or Dad asks that something be done—the kids are to respond in a respectful manner. When a sibling is sharing about his or her day, others are to listen with sincere interest. It is in these and other small matters in the everyday of life that we affirm the personal worth of each individual in the family and model how to treat others in the larger human family.

Different People: Our children will encounter people who seem "different" for one reason or another. We should take advantage of such acquaintances to help our children see that all people deserve our respect and kindness because they are made in God's image and are worthy of honor. Encourage your child to befriend that kid at school who eats lunch alone because others consider him too fat, short, nerdy, slow, poor, etc. Invite a handicapped relative, neighbor, or church member to the house. Build relationships with those of another race, culture, economic status, or generation. In small ways, model with your kids that all people have inherent personal worth.

Planned Activities

Encouragement Float: Place an egg, a glass or jar of water, and a large bowl of salt before each of your children at the table. Tell them that they are going to try to make the egg float in the water. First, place the egg in the water and tell everyone to yell at it. Use shaming phrases such as, "Float, you dumb egg! Are you so lazy you can't even float to the top of the water?" or "What are you, an egg or a mouse?" Make the point that it does no good to treat the egg with disrespect, so try encouragement. One at a time, each child is to stir a couple of spoonfuls of salt into the water while the others take turns saying one encouraging or complimentary thing about that child. Keep it up until the egg begins floating in the water. When everyone has successfully floated his egg (and been encouraged), read Hebrews 10:24-25 together and discuss how treating others with respect and encouragement helps them do better, while disrespect and criticism cause them to sink. (Note: It takes a lot of salt to make this activity work, so be certain you have enough on hand.) (Ages 5–10)

Birthday Celebration: During birthday parties, include time in your celebration for others to share what is special about the birthday child. Celebrate her life and the ways God has made her unique. If your child has a fun sense of humor, celebrate that. If he has an interest in bugs, celebrate that. If she is musical, athletic, creative, studious, giving, adventurous, imaginative, or just plain lovable—celebrate it! Capture the moment and allow everyone in the family to say something affirming to the birthday child on the anniversary of the day God brought him into the world.

Life Mile Markers: We all take pictures and videos of our children during holidays, baseball games, school programs, and other "big" moments. But we rarely take the time to gather the family together around photo albums or the VCR and enjoy viewing these life mile markers together. By spending an evening reviewing the highlights of each person's life, we create an opportunity to celebrate the ways that person is a special blessing to the family, and to the world.

Field Trips

Pay a Visit: A visit to those less fortunate is a wonderful way to accomplish two goals. It helps the children be a blessing to others, and it helps them appreciate their own blessings. Take the children to visit someone in the hospital, the homeless living in a rescue mission, kids who have a parent in prison, or any number of people who are experiencing tough times. Doing so will make a great impact on your children as you model what it means to treat others with respect and compassion, including those whom society has treated as less worthy. Even better, adopt an older person who is shut-in or lives in a nursing home. Regular time spent getting to know the person inside the frail body will show your children that all people are made in God's image and are important!

Play a Part: Another way to help our children see beyond themselves and reinforce the worth of others is to play a part in a missions outreach program. For example, many relief agencies allow you to "adopt" a child, and send you pictures and periodic updates on how your child is progressing and benefiting from the support you send. Involve your children by letting them write letters to the supported child, send gifts, and stay involved in the life of one less fortunate. Most churches also have ways to become involved with the missionary families supported through your missions budget. For those who can afford the time and expense, take a short-term missions trip with the entire family. When we take part in missionary outreach, we reveal God's heart for all people.

A great resource for ideas and tools to help give children a heart for the spiritual needs of people around the world is "The Caleb Project." This organization has a video series for kids on various people groups entitled "Kids Around the World." The videos are 6–7 minutes long and come with an activity pack. They also have a class called "Worldwide Perspectives" for older teens and adults that can be taken as college credit or just for fun. Check out their web site at www.calebproject.org or call (303) 730-4170.

LINK is a free newsletter sharing stories of those who are giving their lives to tell others about Christ. To get on their mailing list write to: The Voice of the Martyrs, P.O. Box 443 Bartleville, OK 74005 (918) 337-8015

Entertainment

Movie Night: Films that can be used to emphasize the worth of each individual include the following.

It's a Wonderful Life: Since most of us watch this wonderful classic every Christmas season anyway, why not take a few moments to discuss the implicit message of George Bailey's life experience? After a lifetime of sacrificing his own dreams and ambitions for the sake of others, George encounters a crisis which pushes him to the edge. Wishing he had never been born, George is visited by an angel named Clarence who shows George what life for others would have been like if not for him. In the end, George realizes just how wonderful life is—all thanks to a little perspective. Here are a few questions to draw out the key lessons of this film.

Question: Why did George wish he had never been born? Answer: Because he was focused on his troubles and on all the things he didn't get to do.

Question: What was so wonderful about George Bailey's life? Answer: He helped a lot of other people.

Question: What is the message of this film? Answer: That we have great worth, even if life doesn't turn out like we expect.

Question: What Bible passage does the life of George Bailey model? Answer: James 1:27.

The Elephant Man: Based upon the true story of a nineteenth-century man named John Merick, this film dramatizes the life of a man who was grotesquely deformed due to a rare disease. After enduring the shame and abuse associated with a traveling freak show, a nurturing doctor brings

John under his care, revealing his rather remarkable intelligence, insight, and sensitivity. In the end, the disease takes John's life, but only after showing the world that he, like others who may appear less worthy, has a spirit made in the image of God. This film is powerful and disturbing, and should be reserved for when the children are a bit older. (Note: Focus on the Family's Adventures in Odyssey has produced an animated adaptation of this story for younger children. It is entitled "In Harm's Way.") Here are a few questions to draw out the key lessons of this film.

Question: Why did most people treat John Merick so badly? Answer: Because they thought he was a freak, less than human.

Question: Why do you think Psalm 23 might have been so meaningful to John? Answer: Because it spoke of God's care and comfort, something John didn't get from other people.

Question: Was John a worthy person, even though he was so ugly to look at? Answer: Yes, he still was made in God's image inside.

Question: What is the lesson to us of this film? Answer: That we should treat others with respect and kindness because they are God's children—no matter how they look.

Marvin's Room: This movie is a touching story of two sisters, Bessie (played by Diane Keaton), who has been caring for her bedridden father (Marvin) and eccentric aunt for twenty years; and Lee (played by Meryl Streep), who has spent the same twenty years messing up her life and the lives of her two sons. Bessie lived a life of self-sacrifice in order to care for others—experiencing love and true meaning in the process. Lee, on the other hand, ran from responsibility and cared only for herself—only to discover that it led to a shallow, conflict-filled existence. *Marvin's*

Room is about their forced reunion after discovering that Bessie has leukemia and may soon die. Have a hanky ready as you watch love break through the conflict to make a powerful statement about the dignity and value of every human life and the meaning that comes from loving the hard to love. Here are a few questions to draw out the key lessons of this film.

Question: By her actions, what was Bessie's view of personal worth? Answer: That all people are worthy and should be treated with dignity, even those who can't care for themselves.

Question: How about Lee? Answer: That we should look out for ourselves only, and accept people who fit into our plan.

Question: In the end, what did Lee learn? Answer: That even though it may be scary, we find true meaning when we put the needs of others above our own.

Question: What does this film say about the worth of the individual? Answer: That we are worthy based upon who we are, not based upon what we do.

Drive Time or Bedtime Audios
Several Adventures in Odyssey and other audio resources address the worth of each individual.

"The Underground Railroad" (AIO episodes #314–316)

"An Encounter with Mrs. Hooper" (AIO episode #72)

"A Mission for Jimmy" (AIO episode #91)

"Pamela Has a Problem" (AIO episode #134) This episode deals with abortion and is not suited for young listeners.

Dinner Table Discussion
What If?:Help your children appreciate the implications of a Christian view of personal worth by contrasting it with the

implications of others' views. Schedule a dinner table discussion in which you ask the following "What if?" questions.

Question: What if Mom and Dad (or God) only loved and accepted the person in the family who did the best at playing marbles? Answer: Most of us would be unhappy and spend all our time trying to become marbles experts.

Question: What if those who became slave traders had believed that all people have personal worth? Answer: They would have opposed rather than promoted slavery.

Question: What if the founding fathers of the U.S.A. had believed Darwin's theory that only the fit should survive? Answer: They would never have built our Constitution on the idea that "all men are created equal. . . ."

Question: What if Adolf Hitler had believed that all people deserved respect because they are created in the image of God? Answer: There would not have been a Holocaust.

→ *Chapter 11* ←

Responsibility

⸙⸙

*T*he clock radio blares at precisely 5:30 A.M., beckoning you to face another day. Requiring only a split second to rationalize away the benefits of morning exercise, you slap the snooze button down, hoping to steal a few extra minutes of sleep. But the knowledge that you must eventually pull back the covers and start the daily routine ruins an otherwise perfect moment. Rather than fight the inevitable, you roll out of bed and begin another tedious day of toil.

What is it that gets us out of bed in the morning? What makes any of us choose to do the mundane and necessary over the fun and frivolous? On the other side of the coin, what is it that causes some to neglect the most basic activities required for wholesome living? One man works sixty hours per week to provide the basic necessities for his family, while another spends thirty hours on the job and drinks away his paycheck. A woman who was mistreated as a child wallows in pain and bitterness, while another who was more severely abused lives a healthy, productive life. What makes the difference?

Perhaps the difference lies in whether or not there is an

understanding of, and commitment to, responsible living. Those who hold themselves accountable for their own choices and attitudes move upstream on the river of life; those who refuse to be held accountable allow themselves to be pulled downstream.

We have seen a gradual change in our society over the past several decades from emphasizing individual responsibility to an emphasis on, and almost glorification of, individual rights. We seem to have replaced the perspective which said, "It's my responsibility" with one which says, "It's your fault!" If things fall apart, there is always someone at whom we can point an accusing finger, relieving ourselves of the burden to properly mend the situation.

This tendency can be seen in the work place, in governmental policies, in civil disputes, in family conflicts, and even in the church. "Give me my rights!" is the battle cry of a new generation. This emphasis can become a primary source of our individual and corporate downfall.

Stay home from work just one afternoon, and you will see numerous television advertisements telling you of your "right" to just compensation for stress at work. A slick lawyer, who is only concerned about your well-being, says "Call 1-800-SUE-THEM and we'll get you what you deserve." As a result, our courts are overburdened and insurance companies are raising rates out of sight. Most unfortunate, however, is the societal perception that an honest day's pay for an honest day's work just ain't good enough anymore!

As parents, it is our job to counter this trend in the lives of our own children. To help them avoid becoming lazy victims, we need to instill in them the what, why, and how of personal responsibility.

What to Understand

The second compass value helps equip our children for the realities of life by accepting personal responsibility for their actions and attitudes. In order to identify true north with regard to personal responsibility, the following should be understood.

Importance: Over the past few decades our culture has undergone a disturbing shift away from individual responsibility toward what *Time* magazine labeled "finger pointers," "crybabies," and "eternal victims." As a result, personal initiative for advancement has been replaced with bellyaching and blame shifting. This is consistent with the natural tendency of man, which is to become passive and irresponsible. We must help our children develop a sense of personal responsibility that will encourage them to overcome, rather than become victims to, the inevitable difficulties of life.

Compass Value: We are responsible for our own actions and attitudes. We must accept the fact that life is difficult for everyone, and blaming other people or circumstances for our problems is foolish. God will bless us as we make right choices.

Supporting Scriptures: The following passages establish the biblical perspective on personal responsibility.

WE ARE RESPONSIBLE FOR OUR ACTIONS AND ATTITUDES
Even a child is known by his actions, by whether his conduct is pure and right (Proverbs 20:11).
For God will bring every deed into judgment, including every hidden thing, whether it is good or evil (Ecclesiastes 12:14).
Do not be deceived: God cannot be mocked. A man reaps what he sows (Galatians 6:7).

LIFE IS DIFFICULT FOR EVERYONE
If you falter in times of trouble, how small is your strength (Proverbs 24:10).
In this world you will have trouble. But take heart! I have overcome the world (John 16:33).

BLAMING PEOPLE OR CIRCUMSTANCES IS FOOLISH

The sluggard says, "There is a lion outside!" or, "I will be murdered in the streets" (Proverbs 22:13).
The complacency of fools will destroy them (Proverbs 1:32).

GOD BLESSES RIGHT CHOICES

He holds victory in store for the upright, he is a shield to those whose walk is blameless, for he guards the course of the just and protects the way of his faithful ones (Proverbs 2:7-8).
Let us not become weary in doing good, for at the proper time we will reap a harvest if we do not give up (Galatians 6:9).

Impression Points _____

Following are several ideas for instilling a sense of personal responsibility in children of various ages. Pick and choose the impression points that will work best for your family.

Real Life Moments

Do Versus Say: It has little impact when we tell our children to be responsible for their attitudes and actions when we fail to model it ourselves. Do your kids hear you pointing the long finger of blame at others (parents, employers, ministers, etc.) for your problems? Do they see you making excuses for your failures rather than taking responsibility for them? If so, you may find it difficult to instill the value of personal responsibility, because more is caught than taught. Do your best to model personal responsibility in the everyday moments of life.

Fess Up! All of us can describe a time or two when we did something irresponsible that we now regret. Whether quitting piano lessons too soon, blaming others for our own foolish decisions, or saying something we wish we hadn't. Take time to share these stories with your children to help them learn from your mistakes.

The Truth of Consequences: One of the hardest things in the world for parents (especially mothers) is to allow their precious little child to learn life lessons the hard way. But sometimes the painful consequences of a given choice can teach the realities of responsibility better than anything we might say. Countless people are trapped in a cycle of irresponsibility in adulthood thanks in large part to a parent who protected them from the consequences of irresponsible choices in childhood. The earlier we allow our kids to suffer the consequences of foolish choices and actions, the easier it will be for them to learn this critical life lesson. Though it may seem harsh, it is the truly loving thing to do. Remember, a wise mother bird pushes the chicks out of the nest so they will learn to fly south for the winter, avoiding starvation in the process.

No Excuse Training: There are certain categories in which you may wish to establish a "No Excuses" policy in your home. When kids bring home grades that are below their potential, do not accept the excuse that the teacher didn't give enough time to get the work done, or gave too many surprise quizzes, or likes the other kids better, or, or, or. . . . When you see your child giving less than 100 percent effort while playing on the team, do not accept the excuse that the coach has favorites or that it isn't an important game. Train your children to take responsibility for their choices and actions regardless of the circumstances they face.

· · · · ·

New Year's Celebration

New Year's Eve at our house is game night. We pull out games the kids want to play, eat pizza, listen to our favorite music, and stay up till midnight to cheer in the new year. The next day we sleep in, have a big breakfast, then take ourselves out to our favorite family restaurant later in the day and talk about what we want to accomplish this year.

S.K. Clovis, CA

· · · · ·

Choices: Children can only learn the impact of choices if they are given the responsibility of making choices on a daily basis. Ask them questions such as the following.

"Do you want to wear your coat or carry it?"

"Is the floor the best place to keep your school backpack?"

"Is whining the best way to communicate what you need?"

"Do you really think it is healthy to have dessert when you didn't eat your meal?"

Such questions let your children know that you believe they can make responsible choices even when they are young. Discuss how they can think through such issues in a responsible manner. By the way, avoid the temptation to give your children warning after warning when they fail to follow through with specific directions. Doing so undermines the consequence principle of responsibility. Set the rules and enforce them right away!

Planned Activities:

Not Fair! One way we convince ourselves that we have a right to be less responsible is by seeing life as unfair. When we get a bum rap, we excuse our irresponsible attitudes and actions. Here is an activity to help undermine this tendency with our kids.

Bring the kids together and divide them into two teams. (The more kids the better, so do this activity when you have friends or relatives over to play. Even if the teams are two kids and two parents, however, it will work.) Tell the teams that you wish to have a little contest between them. Starting with the older kids, give a time limit and offer a reward (a piece of candy, a quarter, etc.) for each time they hit a whiffle ball with a plastic bat (or whatever competitive task would work well for your family). When the second team comes to bat, make the time limit longer, the reward greater, and the task easier. When the first team wins eight quarters for hitting the baseball eight times in thirty seconds, they will be very happy. But when they see you giving the other team one dollar for each successful hit in sixty seconds with easier pitches, they will immediately yell, "Not Fair!" This will provide an ideal opportunity to discuss Jesus' Parable of the Vineyard Workers found in Matthew 20. Just like the workers in the parable, the first team thought they had a great deal until someone else got a better deal; then they thought they had a bum rap. This is like life. We are responsible to make the best of what God gives us without worrying about, complaining about, or comparing to what others are given. (Ages 7–12)

Why Obey? Part of living a responsible life is learning to submit to authority. We must choose to submit or suffer the consequences for failing to do so. In order to reinforce the protective nature of obedience, try these activities.

Have the kids draw a picture of people standing under an umbrella. Write the word "obey" on the umbrella to represent people who are in authority—including parents, God, and others. Draw strong rain coming down around the umbrella, representing the "hard knocks" of life. Explain that people who are in authority are like the umbrella. When we obey them (stay under the umbrella), they protect and keep us safe. But if we disobey (move out from under the umbrella), we can get hurt.

Pull out a real umbrella and have the kids get under it with Mom while Dad stands above them on a ladder or chair. Have several soft objects (rolled up socks, Nerf balls, etc.) to drop on anyone who steps out from under the umbrella. (If you conduct this activity outside, you may want to use a squirt gun or hose!)

Use a stick or a string to create a line on the floor. Place a bowl of goodies several large steps beyond the line. Tell the kids they will be fine as long as they do not cross that line. When they do, nail them with the soft objects!

Once you've had some fun, read 1 Samuel 15:23, Exodus 20:12, and John 14:15 together and discuss the ways our life is better when we learn to be obedient to the authority God places over us. (Ages 5–9)

Can't Take It Back: There is toothpaste all over the plastic-covered table. The kids are having the time of their lives squeezing the paste out of the tube, trying to expunge every drop like Dad told them to. "Okay," says Dad, slapping a twenty-dollar bill onto the table. "The first person to get the toothpaste back into his tube gets this money!" Little hands begin working to shove the peppermint pile back into rolled-up tubes—with very limited success.

"We can't do it, Dad!" protests the youngest child.

"That is just like your tongue," Dad responds. "Once words come out of your mouth, it's impossible to get them back in. So be careful what you say because you may wish you could take it back." An unforgettable impression is made, reinforcing the truth that we are responsible for what we say—for good or bad. (Ages 5–10)

Turn Around: Part of accepting responsibility for our own attitudes and actions is understanding the biblical concept of repentance. Here is a simple way to help our children grasp the idea.

In order to understand "repent," our kids must first understand "sin." Set up several "hit the mark" activities—such as shooting at a toy basketball hoop, hitting Dad with paper wads, playing with a plastic bowling set or Nerf baseball, etc. One at a time, let the kids attempt to score as many points as possible. Each time they miss, however, yell the word "Sin!" without explaining. After several such outbursts, they will likely ask you to explain why you are yelling "Sin!" each time they miss. Answer by reading Romans 3:23 as well as 6:23 and explain that sin is "missing the mark." ("Missing the mark" means not keeping the standard that was set by God—perfection.)

In order to explain "repent," blindfold the children one at a time and tell them to walk in a straight line until they hear you yell, "Repent!" When they hear you yell, "Repent," they need to immediately turn around and start walking the other direction to avoid running into the wall or another object. (For added fun, when Dad takes his turn, he can ignore the shouts and run into the wall—demonstrating the consequences of refusing to repent.) Read Mark 1:4 , 14-15 and explain that repenting is turning away from sin and going the other way.

In summary, when we do something wrong (miss the mark) we need to repent (turn around and go the other way). (Ages 6–10)

Dinner Table Discussion

The Blame Game: Schedule a dinner discussion in which you will play "The Blame Game." Start by reading the first blame game ever played as recorded in Genesis 3. Adam and Eve invented the rules. See if you can identify them as you read.

Rule #1: Make choices based upon what others think.

Rule #2: When caught, blame someone else.

Rule #3: Whatever happens, don't hold yourself responsible for the choice you made.

Once the rules are clear, let each person take turns describing a time when either:

They played the blame game themselves. (Who influenced their choice? How did they blame someone else? Whom did they blame?)

They saw someone else playing the blame game. (What did they blame on whom?)

They realized something was their own fault after blaming someone else.

Once you have had "The Blame Game" discussion, give each other permission to hold one another accountable whenever someone in the family starts blaming others for his own choices or problems by asking, "Are you playing the blame game?"

Drive Time or Bedtime Audios:
Several Adventure in Odyssey and other audio resources
address the theme of responsibility, including:
   "A Victim of Circumstance" (AIO episode #306)
   "Pet Peeves" (AIO episode #268)
   "Mayor for a Day" (AIO episode #153)
   "Eugene's Dilemma" (AIO episode #76)
   "Front Page News" (AIO episode #103)
   "All's Well with Boswell" (AIO episode #125)

Movie Night
Films which can be used to emphasize personal responsibility
include the following.

   A River Runs Through It: In both the book and the film,
this story by Norman Maclean puts a fresh spin on the old
story of two brothers—one generally compliant, the other a
strong-willed prodigal. Though reared by the same loving
mother and a father who is both a Presbyterian minister
and fly fishing fanatic, the boys make very different choices
for their lives and experience very different outcomes.
Touching and tragic, this film paints a clear picture of how
choices bring consequences—good and bad. Here are a few
questions to draw out the key lessons of this film.

   Question: Why did the younger brother (Paul) have a
harder life than the older brother (Norm)? Answer:
Because he made many foolish choices.

   Question: Given the choice between doing what is
responsible or right and doing what is frivolous or wrong,
which would Paul choose? Answer: Frivolous or wrong.

   Question: Did these choices hurt anyone? Answer: Yes,
they hurt himself and his entire family.

Question: What Bible verse does this story illustrate?
Answer: Galatians 6:7-8.

Glory: This powerful film is based upon the true story of
the first black regiment in the Civil War. It focuses on several
men who struggle to gain a sense of dignity after living as
slaves and outcasts. One of the main characters in the story is
an escaped slave named Trip (played by Denzel Washington),
who blames everyone else for his misery. He picks fights,
demeans those around him, and displays a generally sour
attitude. In the end, however, he discovers with the other
men in his regiment that self-respect and honor come to those
who stop blaming the world and start accepting responsibility for doing what is right and honorable. Here are a few
questions to draw out the key lessons of this film.

Question: Why was Trip such an unkind person
throughout much of the movie? Answer: Because he acted
like a tough guy in order to cover up his own misery.

Question: How did he eventually gain some self-respect?
Answer: By joining the others in doing what is right and
honorable.

Question: What was the turning point for him?
Answer: When Sergeant Rolands (played by Morgan
Freeman) made him face how foolish he was being and
encouraged him to join in the prayer and singing service
around the campfire.

Question: Why would this have made a difference?
Answer: Because it helped him see the need to accept
responsibility for changing his attitude.

Adventures in Odyssey Videos
Two children's videos that address the topic of taking responsi-
bility for our actions are:
   A Fine Feathered Frenzy
   A Twist in Time

Systems

Search and Rescue: One of the challenges we face with younger kids is getting them to pick their toys up off the floor. Turn the process into a game by playing "Search and Rescue." Have the child "search" for the lost toys and "rescue" them by placing them where they belong. Work with them to keep it fun. In this small way, we help our kids learn to take responsibility for turning the negative parts of life into something we can have a good attitude about. (Ages 4–8)

Jobs Basket: Create a family jobs basket by placing small sheets of paper describing one task that needs to be done into a basket or jar. Set aside one day per month for completing everything in the basket. Each family member must take turns selecting a job until they are all gone. Plan to treat the entire family to something special that evening once everything is done. (A movie, ice cream, a ride in a convertible sports car, etc.) Some of the jobs will be bigger than others, and certain children may consider their stack unfair. But the rule of the day is "you pick it, you do it." Allow no complaining. This system keeps you caught up on periodic household duties, and it teaches kids that every member of the family must be responsible to pitch in and help. (Ages 7–16)

→ *Chapter 12* ←

Sexuality

༄

*T*he film was intended to make a statement. It features the very different lives of two siblings—brother and sister. He is a nerdy fellow who spends every spare moment watching reruns of his favorite television show. Attracted to the ideal world it presents, the boy dreams of one day living a life as perfect as those in the black-and-white paradise called Pleasantville. She, on the other hand, likes life as it is. Attractive, cool, and popular with the boys—partly because she is willing to sleep around—the last place on earth the sister would want to live is that goody-two-shoes world her geeky brother idolizes. No sir, she prefers life loose and fast—thank you very much.

As the story unfolds, both brother and sister end up in Pleasantville. They, like everyone else, are forced to live in a black-and-white world. It is a world which knows nothing of color or the passion it symbolizes. That is, until the sister decides to educate them on how to "really" have fun!

Before long, teens begin having sex, women leave domineering husbands, and the mother exchanges a mundane marriage for the excitement of an extramarital affair. In short, people begin to experience what life beyond Pleasantville can be. In the process, their black-and-white world gradually turns to brilliant color. Free from the constraints of goody-two-shoes living, the residents of Pleasantville begin to embrace the wonders and excitement of a passion they've never known.

The only problem is a few stick-in-the-mud folks who want to get rid of the "coloreds" and return Pleasantville to the way it was. They liked the world bland and predictable—as it should be! In the end, however, passion wins out and the entire community accepts color as something good.

The statement of the film *Pleasantville* is obvious. "When we free people from the constraints of an outdated value system, they can discover the colorful world of passion. The problem with our culture is not those who promote freedom and sexual expression. The problem is those who would keep us from finding and fulfilling our desires."

There is just one problem with this message. It is completely opposite of reality. Sin, not purity, robs life of passion and color, and turns it into a bland and colorless existence. The short-term thrill of illicit sex is quickly replaced by the guilt and consequences which come when we leave the protective parameters of innocence. Unfortunately, our generation cannot comprehend the wonders of passion fulfilled within the context of purity. It sees any limits on expression as something which steals enjoyment, rather than increases its intensity.

When it comes to sexuality, our children are being fed a lie. It is our job as parents to recognize and counter the lie with the truth of a biblical perspective on sexual identity and passion.

What to Understand

The third compass value speaks to the wonders and dangers of human sexuality. In order to identify true north with regard to sexual identity and passion, the following should be understood.

Importance: Two recent social movements have contributed to a growing disdain for the biblical perspective of human sexuality. With the feminist movement has come confusion over what it means to be distinctly male or female as created by God. The sexual revolution has removed the protective guidelines of sexual expression, confusing love with passion, gratification with fulfillment. The result is a generation trapped in a bland, colorless world, seeking to satisfy a yearning that can only be filled through the wonders of biblical sexuality.

Compass Value: We are created either male or female—each an expression of God's perfect image. Both sexes have unique strengths, passions, and needs designed to be attractive to the other and to be affirmed and fulfilled only within the context of marriage and family life.

Supporting Scriptures: The following passages establish the biblical perspective on sexual passion and identity.

WE ARE CREATED UNIQUELY MALE OR FEMALE

So God created man in his own image, in the image of God he created him; male and female he created them (Genesis 1:27).
This is a profound mystery—but I am talking about Christ and the church. However, each one of you also must love his wife as he loves himself, and the wife must respect her husband (Ephesians 5:32-33).
Husbands, in the same way be considerate as you live with your wives, and treat them with respect as the weaker partner and as heirs with you of the gracious gift of life (1 Peter 3:7).
They exchanged the truth of God for a lie, and worshiped and served created things rather than the Creator. . . . Because of this, God gave them over to shameful lusts. Even their women exchanged natural relations for unnatural ones. In the same way the men also abandoned natural relations with women and were inflamed with lust for one another. Men committed indecent acts with other men, and received in

themselves the due penalty for their perversion (Romans 1:25-27). (Note: The Bible calls sexual behavior that is not heterosexual "unnatural" and "perverse.")

SEXUAL IDENTITY AND PASSION ARE FULFILLED WITHIN MARRIAGE

For this reason a man will leave his father and mother and be united to his wife, and they will become one flesh. The man and his wife were both naked, and they felt no shame (Genesis 2:24-25).

You shall not commit adultery (Exodus 20:14).

But since there is so much immorality, each man should have his own wife, and each woman her own husband. The husband should fulfill his marital duty to his wife, and likewise the wife to her husband. The wife's body does not belong to her alone but also to her husband. In the same way, the husband's body does not belong to him alone but also to his wife. Do not deprive each other except by mutual consent and for a time, so that you may devote yourselves to prayer. Then come together again so that Satan will not tempt you because of your lack of self-control (1 Corinthians 7:2-5).

Impression Points _____

Following are several ideas for instilling a healthy view of sexual identity and passion in children of various ages. Pick and choose the impression points that will work best for your family.

Real Life Moments

Affirming Differences: One of the most important things we can do to give our children a healthy sense of sexual identity is to affirm the differences between sexes. In order to do so, capitalize on critical events in the life of your kids. Dinner and shopping with Mom to celebrate daughter's first bra. A weekend trip to celebrate her "becoming a woman day"—otherwise known as first menstruation. For boys, other events serve as great opportunities to reinforce sexual identity—such as that first hit in a baseball game or first job (whether mowing lawns or a paper route). Take your daughter shopping to buy a frilly new dress when younger or a cute outfit when older so that she can feel feminine and pretty. Bring your son to a professional game and let him admire the strength and aggression that are uniquely masculine and part of the image of God in man. Verbally praise the uniquely masculine or feminine qualities in Dad and Mom in front of the children. Here are some examples.

Dad about Mom: "I think Mom is the prettiest girl in the world. I'm lucky she is my date!" or "Mom has such soft skin. I love to touch it!"

Mom about Dad: "We are blessed to have a Daddy who works so hard." Or "You'll have to ask Daddy to lift that. He is stronger than Mommy."

Special Treatment: We need to model how to treat the opposite sex at home so that our children learn that there are differences which should be respected. For example, make it clear that it is okay to tackle and punch Daddy for fun, but not Mommy. Let your boys know that Mommy or sister deserves privacy when she is changing clothes because she is a girl, and vice versa. Dad should model and enforce with boys to watch their manners when with Mommy and sisters (no burping, gross jokes, etc.). Mom should help teach daughters to be discreet about feminine matters in front of the boys. In these small but important ways, we help our children learn that there is something special about the opposite sex that is worthy of special treatment.

Mush Out: The kids are content. The house is calm. Nothing can disturb this serene setting. Until . . . Dad sneaks up behind Mom, wraps his arms around her waist, and begins blowing in her ear, whispering sweet nothings, and kissing her neck. Before anyone has a chance to stop them, they are embroiled in a full-blown "mush out." The kids react in horror—Mom and Dad are up to it again. The reactions come.

"You guys are gross!"

"Yuck!"

"Not again!"

Translation: It's wonderful knowing that Mom and Dad love one another.

Nothing creates an environment of love more effectively than a Mom and Dad "Mush Out." If you're lucky, the kids may just join in and out-mush the mushers!

Privacy Time: As your children get older and it is more difficult to have evenings alone at home, tell your children that they need to give Mom and Dad privacy for romance and intimacy. Set times in advance that all of the children will need to stay in their bedrooms after a set time (be reasonable, 3:00 P.M. probably won't fly!) to give you private time together. Warn them that if they fail to comply, they might embarrass themselves and you! As with the Mush Out, the kids may complain or tease, but they will love knowing that Dad and Mom are still in love and that sex in the context of marriage is a pure and wonderful gift.

Pornography Protection: One of Satan's most effective tools for undermining the joys and mystery of proper sexuality is pornography. Sadly, we live in an age when it is readily available to children of all ages, whether by a glance at the newsstand in the local convenience store, an innocent search on the Internet, a school buddy who borrows his dad's *Penthouse* magazine, or dialing a voice sex phone number. Pornography is something our kids (boys especially) will encounter in one way or another.

There are two things we must do as parents to help protect our sons and daughters from the destructive and addictive influence of this vice. First, we must shield them during the younger years. How? By staying alert to what they are seeing on cable television, over the Internet, when with friends. By asking them directly whether or not they are being exposed to dirty pictures from buddies, relatives, or other sources. Do not hide your head in the sand on this issue. Stay alert! Second, since it is impossible to be aware of every encounter or influence our children have as they get older, we should have an open and honest discussion about pornography. Mom and Dad should encourage their children (sons especially) to tell them if and when they encounter pornography. We must not react in horror or condemnation. Instead, we should turn such instances into opportunities to discuss the wonder, beauty, and passion associated with sex, and emphasize that we must make it even more exciting by keeping the gift of sensuous nudity wrapped until our wedding night.

Planned Activities

Purity Celebration: Thirteen-year-old Rachael plans to remain sexually pure until her wedding night. She made a formal commitment to that goal at the start of puberty one year ago. Her parents arranged a special ceremony for her, which they called "A Celebration of Purity." The family dressed up, gathered for a formal banquet—the menu and program printed and placed on each plate. The order of celebration included Dinner (featuring Mama), Ceremony (featuring Papa, Mama, Grandpa, Grandma, and close family friends), Special Music, Signing of the Purity Covenant Certificate, and Presentation of a Covenant Gift. With the exception of her actual wedding ceremony, nothing will make a greater impression on Rachael of the beauty and purity of God's design for sexuality.

Letter to Future Spouse: When your children reach the appropriate level of maturity, help them write a letter to the person they hope to marry someday. Encourage them to write about their family, their interests, their hopes and dreams, and about the commitment they are making to remain pure so that they can experience the wonder and excitement of sexual intimacy with him or her alone. This letter can become a powerful symbol and tangible reminder of the importance of remaining pure during the temptation-filled teen years. (Ages 11–15)

Preparing for Adolescence Weekend: Over the past few decades, thousands of parents have confronted the "birds and the bees" discussion in a creative and effective way by acquiring copies of the "Preparing for Adolescence" tapes by Dr. James Dobson. They plan a weekend away—Mom with daughter or Dad with son— and make it a camping trip, a shopping weekend, or whatever the child would enjoy. While driving, parent and child listen to the tapes together—allowing Dr. Dobson to say some difficult things in the hearing of both. This opens up dialogue between parent and child in ways never imagined, yet this dialogue is absolutely critical to prepare early adolescents for the changes they will experience over the coming months and years. You can get a set of "Preparing for Adolescence" tapes from Focus on the Family or from your local Christian bookstore. (Ages 10–15)

. . . . .

Broken Heart

When my oldest son had a broken heart after a breakup with a girl he had been dating, we took the time to talk about God's purpose for relationships before marriage. I stressed the importance of seeing his dating as "courtship" and to consider for future dating a girl he would consider for marriage. He really listened and began to think more seriously about this time as preparation for marriage.

J.J. Clovis, CA

. . . . .

Field Trips
Date Nights: Every few weeks Ken Mason, otherwise known as Daddy, prepares for his date night. He gets spruced up and

heads out to paint the town. But this date is not with Carol, his wife. It is with his teenage daughter Becky. They are heading out to dinner and a movie. Ken will give his daughter tips on proper manners, how to act with boys, and why her purity is a priceless gift. An impression is made. When parent-child date nights are a regularly scheduled activity on the calendar, Mom can take her son out to teach him how to treat a young girl with the respect and admiration she deserves. Or she can take her daughter out to discuss the fine art of appropriate flirting and behaving like a lady. Dad can help his son learn how to make himself look presentable, and discuss how to talk to a girl. In these moments, all kinds of wonderful benefits occur—including planned and unplanned discussions.

Feminine Shopping Outing: Although we all walk past the store lingerie displays pretending that we have no interest in them and would never think of purchasing anything, feminine intimate apparel is a wonderful reality of married life. Why not do the unthinkable and actually take your child with you to purchase something? Mom can take daughter to share the pure excitement of marital intimacy, and to show her that a woman enjoys looking attractive to her husband. Dad can take son to let him know that it is perfectly appropriate and thoughtful to buy your wife a sexy outfit. Certainly be discreet, waiting until the appropriate age and stage of development with your child. But don't miss an opportunity to reinforce the wonder of feminine beauty and the pure thrill of sex within the context of marriage.

Entertainment

Married or Not? When I (Kurt) was young, my mother did something very wise while the family watched television together. Whenever there was a scene in which a man and woman became intimate with one another, my mother would tell us to turn the channel IF the couple was not married. If they were married, on the other hand, we could watch the show. (Incidentally, this was in the days when they were discreet about what was actually shown on television.) In this small way, she made an important statement to help us discern that sex itself is not dirty or wrong, only sex outside the context of marriage.

No Apologies: A wonderful film to show your preteens and teens dealing with the dangers of sex outside marriage is the film entitled *No Apologies* produced by Focus on the Family. A nondramatic but engaging presentation, this film can be a great discussion launcher for you and your adolescent about the hard realities of sexually transmitted disease, unplanned pregnancy, emotional pain, and other consequences of violating God's plan for human sexuality. Copies of this film can be obtained at your local Christian store or by calling Focus on the Family. (Ages 11–16)

Movie Night

There are more romance films than can be counted that are available to help reinforce the wonder of love between a man and a woman. Unfortunately, few recent productions portray romance without sex, and rarely within the context of marriage. You will likely need to look for older films to portray a proper model, and use newer films to point out what is wrong. Here are a few examples.

The Sound of Music: Most of us have seen it several times. *The Sound of Music* is one of the all time best romantic films, portraying the love between Maria (played by Julie Andrews) and Captain Von Trapp (played by Christopher Plummer). Since you likely know the story, we'll move right to some discussion questions to highlight the key themes.

Question: What do you think attracted Maria to Captain Von Trapp? Answer: His strength and character and the loving spirit hidden under his stoic demeanor. Question: What do you think attracted Captain Von Trapp to Maria? Answer: Her delicate and feminine appearance and her playful, nurturing heart.

Question: How does the influence of both impact the children? Answer: Maria gives them fun and nurturing, while the Captain gives them a sense of security and order.

Shadowlands: Based on the true life story of love between C.S. Lewis (played by Anthony Hopkins) and Joy Greshem (played by Debra Winger), this story portrays love between a man and woman that goes deeper than surface romance. It shows a man committed to a woman who has become his wife and soul mate through the process of dying from cancer. A great film to show that there are characteristics other than the physical which draw a man and a woman together, *Shadowlands* models a love more profound than can be found in most modern films. Here are a few questions to draw out the key points of this film.

Question: Why did Joy's first marriage fall apart? Answer: Because her first husband had an affair.

Question: What impact does Joy have on C.S. Lewis (Jack)? Answer: She brings out the best in him, including things he is afraid to face.

Question: What impact does Jack have on Joy? Answer: He gives her the security of unconditional love.

Question: What does Jack get out of caring for Joy? Answer: Nothing—he does it because real love means commitment through the good and bad.

Dinner Table Discussion
How Different: If you want to be politically correct, teach your kids that men and women are essentially the same. If you want to help them develop a healthy respect for the way God created

males and females, point out the wonderful differences between the sexes. Schedule a dinner table discussion in which you examine whether and how men and women are different. Use the Bible passages listed in this chapter as discussion starters, asking each child to share something unique and wonderful about the opposite sex. Some possible questions include the following.

Question: What things do women do better than men? Answer: Nurture, have babies, foster relationships, manage family details, smell good, etc.

Question: What things do men do better than women? Answer: Build things, wrestle, use muscles, play basketball, smell bad, etc.

Question: What do men like about women? Answer: They are soft, sweet, pretty, encouraging, etc.

Question: What do women like about men? Answer: They are strong, stable, hardworking, handsome, kind, etc.

Question: Why do you think God made the sexes different? Answer: To show different sides of Himself.

Personal Stories
How We Started: Kids love to hear the story of how Mom and Dad met, what you liked about each other, funny situations while you dated, fights you may have had, and other details of the fledgling romance between Mom and Dad. Set aside time to tell them your stories!

Mistakes We Made: It is also helpful for us to be honest with our kids about the mistakes we made while dating. If you went too far in your physical relationship, confess to your kids how wrong it was and how it negatively impacted your life. If you became too involved with several people, talk about how hard it was and why you don't want them to make the same mistakes. You may feel like a hypocrite telling them you were a bad model. But remember, there is nothing wrong for a man who broke his arm by falling off a cliff to warn others to stay away from the edge!

Chapter 13

Integrity

∞∞∞

"Mom!" comes the indignant outburst. "I'm not five. I'm six!"

Caught in the act! Trying to save a few bucks by passing your child off as "Five and Under" has backfired. Not only have you offended your child, but you've also embarrassed yourself in front of a complete stranger. You quickly pay the full price and scurry inside the zoo.

We've all been there, done that.

Paying for one salad bar plate and sharing it among three kids.

Pulling into a handicapped parking space because "we will just be a minute."

Stuffing snacks into your child's coat to sneak them past the "No outside food or drinks" sign at the movie theater.

A big deal? Probably not. But each instance reinforces a dangerous message to our kids—that integrity can be hit and miss.

Integrity is living and telling the truth. It is based upon the same word as integration. When we integrate truth into life, we have integrity. It cannot be hit and miss. It cannot be abandoned when convenient. And our kids need to see it modeled by Mom and Dad.

Now that we are all feeling guilty, let's quickly scurry into examining how to instill the value of integrity in our kids.

What to Understand

The fourth compass value relates to living and telling the truth. In order to identify true north with regard to a life of integrity, the following should be understood.

Importance: We live in a society that considers the idea of absolute truth unacceptable, even dangerous. At the same time, we bemoan the breakdown of integrity in our leaders and in the population at large. But we can't have one without the other. True integrity comes when we integrate what we believe into how we live. If truth is relative, then there is no absolute standard for judging right or wrong behavior. We don't tell the truth because we don't live the truth. We have lost integrity because we lost the truth. It is vital that we recapture integrity and instill the value of living and telling the truth in our children.

Compass Value: God reveals the truth, expecting us to incorporate it into every aspect of life. Integrity means integrating the truth into how we live.

Supporting Scriptures: The following passages establish the biblical perspective on integrity.

GOD REVEALS THE TRUTH

I have chosen the way of truth; I have set my heart on your laws. I hold fast to your statutes, O Lord; do not let me be put to shame. I run in the path of your commands, for you have set my heart free (Psalm 119:30-32).

Show me your ways, O Lord, teach me your paths; guide me in your truth and teach me, for you are God my Savior, and my hope is in you all day long (Psalm 25:4-5).

Jesus answered, "I am the way and the truth and the life. No one comes to the Father except through me" (John 14:6).
Sanctify them by the truth; your word is truth (John 17:17).

INTEGRITY IS LIVING THE TRUTH
You shall not give false testimony (Exodus 20:16).
Surely you desire truth in the inner parts; you teach me wisdom in the inmost place (Psalm 51:6).
The integrity of the upright guides them, but the unfaithful are destroyed by their duplicity (Proverbs 11:3).

Impression Points _____

Following are several ideas for instilling integrity in children of various ages. Pick and choose the impression points that will work best for your family.

Real Life Moments

Caught Ya! As the opening guilt trip of this chapter highlights, it is in the small details of life that our theology reveals itself. If we say it is wrong to lie, do we live like it? Can our children observe how we live and draw the conclusion that it is important to live and tell the truth? While none of us is perfect, all of us can make an intentional effort to model what we teach. Why not give our kids permission to say "caught ya!" when we fail to walk consistent with our talk? It may be embarrassing at times. But the long-term lesson is well worth an occasional blush.

Keeping Them Honest: Kids will try to play Mom against Dad in order to get what they want without admitting that one parent already made the unwelcome decision. In order to thwart their wicked intents, it is good to establish a simple little rule to help maintain honesty in the home. When a child asks Dad's permission for something, his immediate response should be, "What did Mom say?" Doing so helps Mom and Dad reinforce one another's leadership in the home, and keeps the kids from getting away with those subtle, early deceptions.

Planned Activities
Seek the Truth: Our two boys are running all over the house, carefully following the complex and challenging instructions spelled out on the "truth treasure map" they received moments ago. An earlier map contained a few rather simple instructions that were much easier to follow. But the "false treasure box" it led to left something to be desired. It was empty. Boo Dad! They hope for a better result with map number two.

Step One: Walk sixteen paces into the front family room.
Step Two: Spin around seven times, then walk down the stairs.
Step Three: Run backward to the other side of the room.
Step Four: Try and get around Dad and climb under the table.

You get the picture. The boys are laughing at themselves, complaining to Dad, and having a ball. After twenty minutes of treasure hunting, they finally reach the elusive "truth treasure box." Little hands open the lid, hoping for a better result this time around. They aren't disappointed. The box contains a nice selection of their favorite candies. Yeah Dad!

"Which map was easier to follow?" Dad asks.

"The first one," comes their response.

"Which one was better?"

"The second one. It led to a true treasure," says the oldest.

"That's just like life." Dad shares, "Sometimes it's easier to follow what is false. But it is always better to seek and follow the truth."

After reading from Proverbs 2 about the hidden treasure of God's truth, the boys recite tonight's jingle, "It's best for you to seek what's true." Then they indulge themselves with a mouthful of delicious candy! (Ages 5–10)

Group Think: Just before your children start another school year, try this little "group think" activity to teach them the importance of remaining faithful to what you know is true, even when others pressure you to do otherwise. Ask one of the children to go into another room and close the door while the rest of the family organizes the activity. On a piece of paper, draw three horizontal lines of slightly different lengths. Label them A, B, and C. Tell the other members of the family that when the other sibling rejoins the group, you are going to ask him to point out which of the three lines is the longest. When he selects the correct line, everyone else will say he is wrong in a united manner. If A is the longest, the group will insist that this is wrong, and ask the child to choose again. After several rounds, the child will either capitulate and select the wrong line, or remain firm and insist he is correct. Either way, reveal the gag and make your point that even if everyone else says something is wrong, we must remain faithful when we know it is right. After leading a discussion about what kinds of things others might try to convince us to do that are wrong, read Proverbs 1:1-2 and 14:12 together and end your time with a little rhyme, "Though everyone might, it may not be right!" (Ages 5–10)

> . . . . .
> ## *Kid's Theater*
> Our girls do a "Kid's Theater" where they act out plays or musicals, usually Bible stories, and present them to us or their friends. They always have a moral to the story.
> *C.W., Brush Prairie, WA*
> . . . . .

Movie Night
Films which can be used to emphasize personal integrity include the following.

Chariots of Fire: Based upon the true story of Eric Liddel, this film portrays the life of a young man whom God gifted with great athletic ability. A devout Christian destined for the mission field, he faces a conflict of integrity when he discovers that the Olympic race for which he has spent a lifetime preparing is scheduled to take place on Sunday—a day he and his family have set apart as sacred. Despite pressure from his future king and other political leaders from his homeland, Liddel insists that he cannot run without violating his deeply held beliefs and personal integrity. His commitment is a model of what it means to live consistent with one's beliefs, even in the face of great sacrifice. Here are a few questions to draw out the key lessons of this film.

Question: Why did Eric refuse to run on Sunday? Answer: Because he believed it was wrong to compete in athletics on the Sabbath.

Question: What did Eric risk by staying true to his belief? Answer: The thing he had prepared his entire life to achieve—an Olympic medal.

Question: What message did Eric's choice send to the world? Answer: That integrity is more important than success.

Quiz Show: In contrast to Eric Liddel's experience, this film dramatizes how subtle and tempting it can be to sacrifice one's integrity for success. Also based upon a true story, this film dramatizes the decision of Charles Van Doren (played by Ralph Fiennes) to accept the answers before competing on a popular game show during the late 1950s. It paints the picture of a man who knows what is right, but rationalizes a little deception in exchange for financial rewards. Here are a few questions to draw out the key lessons of this film.

Question: How did Charles Van Doren rationalize his decision to cheat? Answer: By saying the show was mere entertainment, and that he wasn't hurting anyone else.

Question: How did this decision impact his integrity? Answer: He gradually became more willing to lie.

Question: In the end, who was hurt by Charles Van Doren's deception? Answer: He hurt himself by losing self-respect, and he hurt his family by undermining their reputation.

Question: What passage of Scripture does this film illustrate? Answer: Proverbs 11:3.

Dinner Table Discussion

What Do They Believe? Hold a dinner table discussion in which you examine what people really believe based upon how they live and the choices they make. Preface the discussion by reading Proverbs 11:3 and sharing that the Bible tells us our integrity should guide our actions, and that how we live is a reflection of what we believe. Ask children to share their thoughts in response to questions like these.

Question: John calls in sick to work when he wants to golf instead. What does he believe? Answer: That it is okay to deceive others in order to do what we want.

Question: Martha takes several boxes of paper clips home from the office because she ran out. What does she believe? Answer: That it is okay to steal.

Question: Frank demeans his wife and children and treats them with disrespect. What does he believe? Answer: That he is more important than others are, and that people are not worthy of respect.

Question: Lisa failed to study, so she cheats on an exam. What does she believe? Answer: That it is okay to lie in order to get ahead in life.

Such questions reinforce the reality that integrity means integrating what we believe into how we live, and that what we say is not nearly as important as what we do.

Drive Time or Bedtime Audios

Several Adventures in Odyssey and other audio resources address the theme of personal integrity, including the following.

"It Takes Integrity" (AIO episode #181)

"The Election Deception" (AIO episode #284)

→ Chapter 14 ←

Discipline

*n his best-selling book entitled *The Road Less Traveled*, M. Scott Peck, M.D., describes a principle he calls "delayed gratification" and how it should develop in the lives of our children.

> *Delayed gratification is the process of scheduling the pain and pleasure of life in such a way as to enhance the pleasure by meeting and experiencing the pain first and getting it over with. It is the only decent way to live.*
>
> *This tool or process of scheduling is learned by most children quite early in life, sometimes as early as age five. For instance, occasionally a five-year-old child when playing a game with a companion will suggest that the companion take first turn, so that the child might enjoy his or her turn later.*[1]

Peck goes on to describe what should be the normal pattern of learned discipline in children—from a child aged six eating the cake first and the frosting last, to a twelve year old taking it upon himself to finish his homework before watching television. But many children, according to educators, do not learn this discipline—with serious life consequences. " 'Play now, pay later,' is their motto. So the psychologists and psychotherapists are called in. But most of the time, it seems too late."[2]

Why is it that some fail to learn the process of delayed gratification? Why do some children mature into well-adjusted, self-disciplined young people, while others fall into continual patterns of self-subversion? According to Peck "most of the signs rather clearly point to the quality of parenting as the determinant."[3]

The lesson is simple: If we expect our children to become self-disciplined later in life, we must begin the process of teaching discipline early in life.

What to Understand

The fifth compass value relates to hard work and self-discipline. In order to identify true north with regard to discipline, the following should be understood.

Importance: One of the most important learned skills for success in life is delayed gratification through personal discipline. Yet, ours is an impatient culture, unwilling to work or wait for anything. Immediate gratification has become an expectation, even a right. As parents, we often feed this tendency by giving our children whatever they want, whenever they want it—setting them up for failure down the road. By instilling a strong work ethic and sense of stewardship, however, we can help them develop the discipline needed to rise above and become a leader in a world filled with the self-indulged.

Compass Value: Good things come to those who are willing to work and wait. Discipline is the ability to put off immediate pleasures for something even better down the road.

Supporting Scriptures: The following passages establish the biblical perspective on discipline.

BE WILLING TO WORK AND WAIT
How long will you lie there, you sluggard? When will you get

up from your sleep? A little sleep, a little slumber, a little folding of the hands to rest—and poverty will come on you like bandit and scarcity like an armed man (Proverbs 6:9-11). *All hard work brings a profit, but mere talk leads only to poverty* (Proverbs 14:23).

For even when we were with you, we gave you this rule: "If a man will not work, he shall not eat." We hear that some among you are idle. They are not busy; they are busybodies. Such people we command and urge in the Lord Jesus Christ to settle down and earn the bread they eat (2 Thessalonians 3:10-12).

PUT OFF IMMEDIATE FOR SOMETHING BETTER

Go to the ant, you sluggard; consider its ways and be wise! It has no commander, no overseer or ruler, yet it stores its provisions in summer and gathers its food at harvest (Proverbs 6:6-8).

Lazy hands make a man poor, but diligent hands bring wealth. He who gathers crops in summer is a wise son, but he who sleeps during harvest is a disgraceful son (Proverbs 10:4-5). *The sluggard craves and gets nothing, but the desires of the diligent are fully satisfied* (Proverbs 13:4).

Impression Points _____

Following are several ideas for instilling self-discipline in children of various ages. Pick and choose the impression points that will work best for your family.

Real Life Moments

A Two-Letter Word: There is a word that every child dreads, but that every parent needs to learn. It is a simple, two-letter word that can make the difference between kids who are spoiled and ill-equipped for real life, and kids who have learned that the world will not jump at their beck and call. It is the word NO.

During the early years, they need to hear it periodically from Mom and Dad. Not always. Not harshly. But they do need to learn from us that they cannot have everything they want. It will happen as you pass the grocery store aisle with the colorful box of sugar-filled cereal with a special offer inside. The kids will ask, then plead, then beg, then demand that you get it for them. Say no and stick to your guns. It will happen as you are standing in line waiting to pay too much for too few items and they spot the candy bar display. They will whine, throw tantrums, and embarrass the living daylights out of you. Say no and make them regret making a scene when you get home. Parents who can't say no to their kids when younger face the potential heartache of grown kids who believe the world should give them what they want, when they want it. So start your kids on the right path. Let them hear that powerful little word now and then—NO.

The Long Lost Joblet: Once upon a time, boys and girls across America learned how to build a business and work hard by signing up to carry papers. But paper routes and other "joblets" are becoming a thing of the past. Papers once carried by paperboys have become drive routes, taking away one of the most effective tools for a parent to help kids learn self-discipline and hard work. Still, there are some joblets available if you keep an eye out for them, such as mowing neighborhood lawns, shoveling snow, raking leaves, etc. There are even a few kid paper routes left in the world. So keep a lookout for a joblet that your child can adopt as a tool for learning the rewards and challenges of work. But be warned. Behind every successful kid with a paper route or other joblet is an always persistent, sometimes nagging parent. Be ready to motivate (or threaten) your child during those times he is tempted to become irresponsible or lazy.

Take a Day Off: On a day when you really can afford to not get much done, take a day off. Don't make breakfast, don't make your bed, don't clean up after yourself etc. Take that opportunity to show how the small daily disciplines of life are important. (Be ready for some big complaints from the ones who are usually benefiting from all that gets done around the house.)

Pay Off: Be sure to capture the moment when long-term discipline finally shows a pay off by celebrating the accomplishment and emphasizing the benefits of discipline. After your children play in a piano recital (mistakes and all) or a sports game, take them out to celebrate the discipline of practice that is required to do so. When he or she finishes a school project that required many hours of investment, celebrate the discipline necessary to have completed the task. In these small ways, we reinforce the connection between personal discipline and the rewards of life.

Planned Activities
Stewardship Blocks: To teach your kids the importance of being good stewards of their time, cut a piece of wood into eight to ten blocks of various sizes. Make sure the total length when laid end to end is greater than the length of a household coffee or dining table. On each block, write one of the following words representing the various activities that could fill time in the child's day— doing chores, sleeping, eating, going to school, playing computer games, watching television, reading, bathing, etc. Write the less important items (television, computer games, etc.) on the shorter blocks, and the essential items (eating, sleeping, etc.) on longer blocks. Invite the kids to the "24 Hour" table and ask them to place the blocks on the table in order of what they like to do.

Your children will quickly discover that there is not enough room on the table for several of the really important blocks. Discuss the items left over, and ask what the impact on life would be if there were not enough time to eat, bathe, go to school, etc. Next, ask them to place the blocks on the "24 Hour" table in order of importance. They will find that several of the "like to do" blocks will not fit on the table. Share that this is like life. Point out that we have a limited amount of time, and we must carefully select and prioritize how we will spend that time, making certain to do the important things before the fun things. There will be time for all the fun things, but maybe not on every day. Read Ecclesiastes 3:1 and the parable in Matthew 25:14-29 and discuss ways to implement this principle in your home. (Ages 5–10)

Rolling in Money: Kids have a hard time understanding the value of money. One day, I (Kurt) went to the bank and withdrew 1,000 one-dollar bills from our savings account. (Yes, they gave me funny looks.) I very carefully took the pile of money home and created a large money pile hidden behind some large boxes in the play area. We blindfolded the children and led them into the room, removed the blindfolds, and told the kids to find the secret treasure. After looking around, they finally found the cash pile and promptly went nuts! "We're rich! We're rich!" they shouted while throwing money in the air and rolling in cash.

We instructed the kids to count the cash to let us know how much we had. Deep within the pile, I placed an envelope labeled "Special Stewardship Instructions" for the kids to discover. The envelope contained three Bible passages with instructions on how to use the money. The kids were told that they could spend everything that remained after we met our stewardship requirements.

Malachi 3:10 = Give 10 percent to God.

Proverbs 30:24-25 = Save 10 percent for the future.

Romans 13:8 = Pay your bills. (Several pretend bills were listed, such as $500 for the house payment, $150 for food, $150 for the car, etc.)

Once the large cash pile was counted and broken into smaller Give, Save, and Bills piles, we counted the remaining money. Each child was given $1 to spend. Needless to say, they were a bit disappointed. But they also better understood the real world expenses of life, and our responsibilities as stewards of the money God gives. We ended our time together by creating a "Stewardship Box" with three slots labeled Give, Save, and Spend for the kids to use when they earn money, and by memorizing our little jingle for the evening, "Before you spend away—give, save, and pay." (Ages 5–10)

Endurance: If you are really nuts, try this activity. Place a large bucket of melted snow and ice with several dozen marbles in the bottom in front of your children. Tell the kids that you will pay a quarter for every marble each child can pull out of the water with his or her toes in three minutes or less. If your children are at all greedy, they will jump at the opportunity to torture themselves for a few minutes in order to reap the rewards of several dollars. Once completed, ask the kids (who will likely be holding blue feet) to explain why they did such a painful thing. "For the money" will come the reply. "So you looked beyond the short-term pain in order to gain the long-term reward?" Point made. When we look beyond the short-term pain or inconvenience of doing what is hard, we can reap the rewards that come from self-discipline and delayed gratification! (Ages 5–12)

Long-Term Project: A simple way to reinforce the value of delayed gratification is to plan a long-term project as a family that will require several weeks or months to complete a little at a time, such as building a toy box, painting the basement, landscaping the yard, or organizing the garage. Identify a reward for the entire family once the task is completed, such as a camping trip, attending a professional ball game, or some activity that will motivate everyone. Once completed, enjoy the anticipated reward together in celebration of the commitment and discipline required to succeed.

Workplace Visit: Many companies schedule an annual "take your child to work" day. Take advantage of these opportunities to let your kids see what you do, and to discuss what it means to commit to a job as well as the expectations and rewards of professional excellence.

Personal Stories

The Rewards of Discipline: If you take the time to reflect, you will discover several stories from your own experience that can be told to your children to illustrate the rewards of discipline and hard work. For example, I (Kurt) tell the story of when I was a paperboy growing up in Michigan. During a particularly severe winter blizzard, the roads and lawns between houses were blown over with several feet of snow. When I arrived at a house near the end of my route, I discovered there was a snowdrift as tall as myself blocking the front door. I seriously considered skipping that house rather than digging my way to the door. But I thought better, plunged forward, and eventually found the front door. Just as I pulled the outer door open to place the paper inside, the inner door swung open from within and the lady of the house handed me a $5 bill (a lot of money in those days). She said, "I told my husband, if that kid gets us the paper today, he deserves an extra special tip!" That experience was a great reminder that in big and small ways, going the extra mile pays off!

> . . . . .
>
> ## Truth in Advertising
>
> My daughter picked up from a political TV commercial that one candidate cared about schools and another one didn't. I had to explain to her that you can't always believe the commercials exactly as they are worded on television. Of course, this led to a discussion on telling the truth and being careful repeating things you hear.
>
> *D.H. Colorado Springs, CO*
>
> . . . . .

Will I Wish I Had? There are times in life when the theory of delayed gratification must become a hard reality. When facing the prospect of three additional years of graduate school in order to earn a masters degree, (I) Kurt wrestled with the financial and time commitment it would require. Newly married and eager to start buying furniture, a car, and maybe a house like all my friends, I saw the long road of graduate school as an obstacle to those short-term goals. Someone I admire asked me to consider a very important question when confronted with such choices. He asked, "Looking back ten years from now, will you wish you had done it?" The answer was clear. "Yes, I would regret it later if I don't get the degree." Ever since, I have counseled young people trying to make a decision involving delayed gratification to ask themselves that same question. As you counsel your own children as they mature, share the times you made a decision that seemed very difficult at the time, but that you would have regretted had you made a different choice. Encourage them to consider what they will wish they had done later, rather than what they may want to do now.

Entertainment

The Olympic Games: Both the winter and summer Olympic games are a perfect opportunity to enjoy great entertainment that can inspire your children with the experience of other young people who have become the best as a reward for great personal discipline. Usually, the networks profile some of the more dramatic stories of personal triumph and sacrifice, providing you with an opportunity to discuss what it means to live a disciplined life.

Movie Night

Films, which can be used to emphasize the rewards of personal discipline, include the following.

    Rudy: Based on the true story of Dan "Rudy" Ruettiger, this film is a powerful picture of determination to accomplish the unlikely through personal discipline and hard work. A poor student and mediocre athlete, Rudy has a dream of someday playing football for the University of Notre Dame. Four years after high school graduation, Rudy finds himself working in the steel mill with his father and brother, his dream unrealized. After an accident that takes the life of his best friend, Rudy heads to South Bend to pursue his dream, only to discover his grades are inadequate to get into Notre Dame. As this inspiring story unfolds, Rudy disciplines himself to overcome incredible obstacles in order to reach his goal. Here are a few questions to draw out some key lessons of this film.

Question: What were some obstacles Rudy had to overcome to achieve his dream? Answer: Poor grades, being small, being poor, a family that didn't believe in him, etc.

Question: What were the most important qualities Rudy displayed in order to overcome each of these obstacles? Answer: Determination, self-discipline, and hard work.

Question: What was so special about his accomplishment? Answer: He gained a sense of self-respect, and he broke out of the cycle of complacency his family was trapped in.

Question: What Bible passage does this film illustrate well? Answer: Proverbs 13:4.

Iron Will: Also based upon a true story, this movie is about the quest of a young man named Will Stoneman who entered and won a dangerous dog sled race across the frozen Canadian wilderness. A dramatic story of determination and discipline, *Iron Will* is a great film to launch the family into a discussion on the challenges and rewards of personal discipline. Here are a few questions to draw out some key lessons.

Question: Why did Will want to win the race so badly? Answer: Because he needed the money to save the family farm.

Question: Why didn't he take the easy way and accept money to quit the race? Answer: Because he wanted to accomplish his goal in a noble manner rather than by cheating.

Question: What lessons can we take from Iron Will's experience? Answer: That we can accomplish great things if we discipline ourselves.

Drive Time or Bedtime Audios

Adventures in Odyssey resources which address the theme of discipline include the following.

"Making the Grade" (AIO episode #264)
"The Secret Keys of Discipline" (AIO episode #271)

Dinner Table Discussion

The Job Interview: Set aside one dinnertime discussion session to have your children place themselves in the shoes of an employer who is looking for a good worker. Create a list of different careers and jobs, and on each one ask your children to describe what qualities they would look for in the person they want to hire. Keep a list of similar themes that should emerge with every role, such as being on time, working hard, being friendly and obedient, etc. You may even want to role play with the children by pretending to be a job applicant and answering questions they create for you. Use this discussion to reinforce the qualities we should strive to build into our own lives.

Systems

Time Coupons: In order to help your children develop a habit of discipline and delayed gratification with regard to how they invest their time, try the time coupon system. Create a set of coupons worth thirty minutes each for watching television, playing computer games, etc. Allow the kids a total of perhaps three hours per week (or whatever you deem appropriate), and give them the appropriate number of coupons at the start of the week. Whenever they wish to spend time on one of these activities, they must pay you one coupon, which reduces the remaining allotted time for the week. Once the coupons are gone, they can spend no more time on these activities unless they earn more through special chores, practicing piano, or some other extra effort.

Weekly Allowance: Many parents struggle with the idea of giving their children an allowance, because they are concerned it may give children the wrong message about chores. They feel it is a child's duty to carry his own load around the house without getting paid. We agree. There are some duties which should simply be part of life. However, a weekly allowance is a very effective system for teaching our children how to be good stewards of money. So we recommend establishing some type of regular system in which your children earn money from an early age so that you can help them establish good habits of giving, saving, and spending.

Cash in Hand: To help your children learn delayed gratification with regard to money, establish a rule that the kids can only spend money on an item they want when they have the cash to do so. This will develop a pattern of learning the discipline and rewards of saving money until there is enough for an important purchase, rather than wasting it on little things and "borrowing" from Mom and Dad to buy the big stuff. This is a very important and difficult habit to learn in a culture that has gone wild with credit spending. All the more reason to instill the discipline when our children are young.

⇥ *Chapter 15* ⇤

On Purpose

〜〜

*T*here was a familiar voice on our answering machine.
The message was brief, but pregnant with concern.

"Hi, Kurt and Olivia. This is Rob. Could you give us a call
as soon as you get home? Shelly and I need to get your advice
on how to handle something."

Rob and Shelly were members of our church. We had been
friends for years. Their boys were about the same ages as ours.
A nice family.

"Hi, Rob, this is Kurt. What's up?"

Rob proceeded to describe a disturbing situation involving
Peter, his nine-year-old. Both Rob and Shelly reacted, perhaps
overreacted, when they discovered their son and an older friend
behaving in an inappropriate manner earlier that day. They were
doing something that reflected preadolescent sexual curiosity. Rob
and Shelly were caught off guard. Lacking confidence about what
to do or how concerned they should be, they called for advice.
After attempting to assure Rob that the incident does not mean his
child is a sexual deviant, I recommended the name of a counselor
who might be able to give some perspective on such issues.

The next day, Shelly called to discuss the situation with Olivia. Still shaken, she began to question the job they were doing as parents. With two younger children, one with severe health problems, there was no time to do anything of a spiritual nature as a family. To make matters worse, they were somewhat passive and permissive with regard to what they allowed the kids to watch on television and video. Both were feeling guilty and inadequate.

"Shelly, you guys are so busy that you probably find yourself constantly reacting to the things your kids say and do, and not being proactive with them. Is that right?" Olivia had hit the nail on the head.

"We find ourselves shocked at what our kids say and do, what they believe and don't believe," came Shelly's response. "The other day, we asked Peter how we get to heaven, and he responded, 'By being good.' We have been taking him to church his entire life, and he should know that it is by believing in Jesus. We were shocked!"

Rob and Shelly's experience is all too common. We take our kids to church, teach them a few bedtime prayers, and hope that everything else falls into place. Sadly, without more intentional effort, it won't. Remember, there is a deceiver at work seeking to seduce our kids. He has had thousands of years to perfect his craft, and has more forms of influence today than ever before. We must be more diligent than any generation in history.

The good news is that Rob and Shelly responded well to this mini-crisis. They sought and implemented advice on how to deal with the incident. More importantly, they took it as a wake-up call and moved from accidental, reactive parenting to being intentional and purposeful in the spiritual development of their kids. As a result, little Peter is getting more attention and investment than ever, and it shows!

On Purpose _____

Take a moment to reflect upon the last few months. Were you busy? Too busy? Did you have unexpected interruptions— perhaps sick kids, unplanned phone calls, nagging headaches, or car trouble? Were there last-minute assignments at work, special church meetings, parent-teacher conferences, soccer practices, music lessons, dentist appointments, and a hundred other activities that filled up your calendar? If so, your home is much like ours.

Now ask yourself this. Do you honestly think it will be much different during the next few months?

How about the next year?

How about the next ten years?

Let's face it, hurry and overcommitment are part of life. There is nothing on the horizon that will magically take away all the activity or give us a thirty-two-hour day. So more than ever, we must become intentional about

. . . . .

Mom's Turn

Memorizing Bible verses is part of our son's homework each week. He would often get frustrated when I would make him repeat the verse when he would make a mistake. Then one week after he had made his attempt at the verse, I suggested "Okay. Mom's turn." He enjoyed the challenge, as well as drilling me and watching the blank expression on my face when I'd forget the next phrase.

G.A. Blue Jay, CA

. . . . .

teaching our children the values we consider important. It is not a matter of when we will have the time, but rather a question of if we will take the time to make a plan.

In this chapter, we are going to combine all we've learned regarding theory and principles, and about teaching our children Christian values, to create an intentional plan for doing so. In the process, we hope to become "on purpose" parents.

Game Plan

Before jumping in with both feet, we must create a very intentional plan of action. Many of us spend more time planning our
vacations, which last one week per year, than we do planning
the spiritual training process for our children, which will last for
eternity. Draw upon the ideas given in chapters five through
fourteen as you complete the following four-step outline that is
designed to move you from accidental to purposeful parenting.
Remember, there will never be a time in life when you have
plenty of extra time to become intentional. By spending a few
proactive hours now and then, you can develop a plan that will
provide you with impression points for several months or more.

Step One: Assess

The first step in becoming intentional is to assess the present situation. In business terms, you must define the "as is" before you are
ready to move toward the "to be." Answer the following questions
which are designed to help clarify your current situation.

1. AM I INTENTIONAL?

On a scale of one to ten, how would you rate your level
of intentionality thus far in the spiritual development
of your children? (1 = "we drop them off at church";
10 = "we conduct planned spiritual training activities
every week with our children.")

1   **10**

2. DO I HAVE A TARGET?

Identify three faith-related values and three character
values you intentionally try to instill in your children.

_____

_____

_____

_____

_____

_____

_____

_____

_____

_____

_____

_____

3. DO I HAVE A PLAN?

Briefly describe the plan you are following for the spiritual development of your children. Include goals, activities that support those goals, and a brief description of three successful activities.

_____

_____

_____

_____

_____

_____

_____

_____

_____

_____

_____

4. AM I EFFECTIVE?

There is a difference between activity and impact. Rate
the level of impact your plan has had on the beliefs and
behaviors of your children. (1= "they haven't learned a
thing"; 10 = "they could teach other children what
they've learned.")

```
1                                                      10
```

5. ARE THEY LEARNING?

In the process of giving our children a solid grasp of a
Christian worldview, we need to rate their level of understanding. From time to time, it is important to assess what
they do and don't understand. In the space provided,
briefly describe your read on your child's current level of
understanding with each of the values you have been
attempting to instill as listed above.

_____

_____

_____

_____

_____

_____

_____

_____

_____

_____

_____

If you are like most of us, this assessment made you very uncomfortable. It has revealed that good intentions may not be getting the job done. Before the guilt and shame overwhelm us, let's quickly move on to the second step in the process.

Step Two: Aim

The second step in becoming intentional is to aim. Random acts of instruction are better than nothing, but it is far more effective to focus your efforts with a predefined objective. It is helpful to define the "to be," that place you want to move toward over the coming twelve months. The following process is designed to help you focus your value-teaching efforts to close the gap between what your children presently understand and the values you consider most important for them to grasp.

1. **SET THE TARGET:** Assuming the goal is to help your children understand the basics of Christian faith and character, use the values described in chapters five through fourteen as a benchmark for creating your target. Again, while this list is by no means exhaustive, it provides a good starting place.

We must ask ourselves what we want our children to understand as they grow, and become intentional about the process of instilling those values. As a starting point, create a notebook in which you define your target in the compass giving process. Use a similar format to the following example.

Child: Shaun
Age: Six
Topic: Who is Satan?
Target Belief: I would like Shaun to understand that there is a real enemy called Satan who is a liar and whom God will defeat.

2. MEASURE THE IMPACT: Develop a habit of evaluating the impact your plan is having with your children to avoid fruitless activity. How many parents, out of guilt, conduct family devotions which have little to no spiritual impact on their children? To avoid this all-too-common pattern, we encourage you to measure the impact of your efforts.

The best way to measure your impact is to compare what you want your children to understand to what they actually do understand. Just as a schoolteacher tests his or her students to assess the impact of instruction, we parents should periodically evaluate what our children are and aren't learning. Comparing what our kids know to the target we've established can keep us focused on results rather than just activity.

Now for the painful part of the process. Periodically, ask your child a few questions in order to assess his or her level of understanding. (By the way, it is best to do so in a fun manner—such as by creating a game of Jeopardy—so that the child doesn't feel he or she is on the hot seat.) For example . . .

Child: Shaun
Age: six
Topic: Who is Satan?
Questions:
Shaun, who is Satan?
Is he good or bad?
Does he tell the truth or lies?
Is he as strong as God?

3. ESTABLISH THE PRIORITY: Compare what your child understands to the target you set. This periodic evaluation will help you determine which values and activities need the most time and effort over the coming months. Based upon your initial assessment, list the six values that you intend to emphasize first. If none stand out above the others, we recommend starting with the six compass beliefs (Who is God?, Is the Devil real?, What is the Bible?, Who am I?, and Why believe in Jesus?).

After you have evaluated the gaps between "to be" and "as is," it is time to turn good intentions into an action plan. This moves us to step three in the process.

Step Three: Act

Now it is time to act, to take that all-important step of pulling out the family calendar and protecting the time to make it happen. That's right, the calendar. If the goals, concepts, and activities you've identified don't find their way onto the everyday calendar you use to run family affairs, they will not happen. Again, good intentions won't get it done. But specific activities on the calendar, with a plan of action behind them, will put you on the road toward being intentional. There is nothing mystical or necessarily profound about teaching our children Christian values. It is a discipline, not a talent. Getting it on the calendar is a vital step along the path of making the goal a reality, and turning "someday" into "today."

By completing this section, you will have taken the most important step in the process of becoming on-purpose with regard to teaching your child Christian values. We have given a few examples below. Of course, you can revise and redo this plan from time to time. We simply want to help get you started.

Drawing from the concepts and ideas in chapter five and beyond, list two or more value-passing activities you will conduct in each of the following twelve months. You may want to select a different theme, belief, or value for each month. Follow the example given.

MONTH: JUNE

Activity #1

Compass Belief: *Our Sin Nature*
Target Child: *David, Age 14*
Date: *July 12*
Summary: *We will read Romans 3:10-18 and watch the movie* Lord of the Flies *together as a set up for discussing the impact of the human sin nature and how it drives all of us to evil if left unchecked.*

MONTH: JULY

Activity #1

Compass Value: *Self-Worth*
Target Child: *Kyle, Age 8*
Date: *July 25*
Summary: *We will use Kyle's birthday as an opportunity to emphasize his own worth to us and God by conducting an "In God's Image" family night activity.*

Once you have completed this exercise, be sure to protect the time and date on the calendar in order to avoid scheduling yourself away from the game plan.

"Put Their Trust in God"

Let's return for a moment to the first principle in our theology of parenting. The Legacy Principle says that what we do today will directly influence the multi-generational cycle of family traits, beliefs, and actions—for good or bad. For many of us, this is a moment of truth, one in which we will choose between the good and the bad. Will we obey the command to teach our children, or abdicate that responsibility to the church, school, and culture? We invite you to join us as we seek to reap the benefits described in Psalm 78.

We will not hide them from our children; we will tell the next generation the praiseworthy deeds of the Lord, his power, and the wonders he has done. He decreed statutes for Jacob and established the law in Israel, which he commanded our forefathers to teach their children, so the next generation would know them, even the children yet to be born, and they in turn would tell their children. Then they would put their trust in God and would not forget his deeds but would keep his commands. They would not be like their forefathers—a stubborn and rebellious generation, whose hearts were not loyal to God, whose spirits were not faithful to him (Psalm 78:4-8).

→ Conclusion ←

When You Lie Down

ⵞⵏⵏⵏ

I t is 9:30 P.M. Well past bedtime. Even though it is late, I (Olivia) am keeping my promise to lie on the bottom bunk next to eight-year-old Kyle and talk before the boys fall asleep. Shaun, our six year old, is on the top bunk. Despite the inability to see my face due to the darkness, he peers over the edge to ask me a very profound question.

"Mom, we are supposed to love everybody, right?"

"That's right sweetie." I respond, unaware that I am being set up.

"What about Satan? Are we supposed to love Satan?"

I don't quite know the proper theological response, so I go with my gut instinct.

"No! We aren't supposed to love Satan!"

Naïvely confident I've satisfied a six-year-old question, Kyle chimes in to spoil my moment. "Yes we are, Mom! We're supposed to love everybody—we just aren't supposed to love what he does."

Wondering whether or not I'm qualified for this compass passing role, I fumble for something to end the conversation so we can all get to sleep.

"Well, are we or aren't we?" Shaun needs an answer right

now or he will be up all night.

"We'll talk about it later. Now go to sleep." I say in a firm yet loving manner.

Lovely silence for about sixty seconds.

"If Satan was an angel who sinned, can other angels sin?" Kyle raises the bar.

Now I'm in real trouble. Where do they get these questions? What ever happened to the days when "Now I lay me down to sleep" covered things?

"Ask your daddy to explain that one during family night." Whew!

Tomorrow Kurt and I will need to discuss both questions, figure out the biblical answer, figure out how to bring it down to their level, and schedule a family night on the topic of Satan. Of course, after we've done all that, they will have an even tougher question to trigger the entire process all over again.

The compass passing process can be challenging, exhausting, and often intimidating. The questions never stop. The task is never done. Their little hearts look to us for answers to life. We wonder whether we are up to the task.

But if we don't do it, who will?

Future generations are waiting for us to start the cycle, to teach them the values that will give them an anchor for living. As we look back from eternity, may we hear that our children, grandchildren, and beyond "put their trust in God" thanks to the effort we put forth today.

On behalf of future generations, thank you for making an effort to teach your children Christian values!

Impress them on your children. Talk about them when you sit at home and when you walk along the road, when you lie down and when you get up. Tie them as symbols on your hands and bind them on your foreheads. Write them on the doorframes of your houses and on your gates (Deuteronomy 6:6-9).

How to Lead Your Child to Christ

Some things to consider ahead of time:

1. Realize that God is more concerned about your child's eternal destiny and happiness than you are. "The Lord is not slow in keeping his promise. . . . He is patient with you, not wanting anyone to perish, but everyone to come to repentance" (2 Peter 3:9).

2. Pray specifically beforehand that God will give you insights and wisdom in dealing with each child on his or her maturity level.

3. Don't use terms like "take Jesus into your heart," "dying and going to hell," and "accepting Christ as your personal Savior." Children are either too literal ("How does Jesus breathe in my heart?") or the words are too clichéd and trite for their understanding.

4. Deal with each child alone, and don't be in a hurry. Make sure he or she understands. Discuss. Take your time. A few cautions:

   1. When drawing children to Himself, Jesus said for others to "allow" them to come to Him (see Mark 10:14). Only with adults did He use the term "compel" (see Luke 14:23). Do not compel children.

2. Remember that unless the Holy Spirit is speaking to the child, there will be no genuine heart experience of regeneration. Parents, don't get caught up in the idea that Jesus will return the day before you were going to speak to your child about salvation and that it will be too late. Look at God's character-He is love! He is not dangling your child's soul over hell. Wait on God's timing. Pray with faith, believing. Be concerned, but don't push.

The Plan:

1. God loves you. Recite John 3:16 with your child's name in place of "the world."

2. Show the child his or her need of a Savior.

a. Deal with sin carefully. There is one thing that can not enter heaven—sin.

b. Be sure your child knows what sin is. Ask him to name some (things common to children—lying, sassing, disobeying, etc.). Sin is doing or thinking anything wrong according to God's Word. It is breaking God's Law.

c. Ask the question "Have you sinned?" If the answer is no, do not continue. Urge him to come and talk to you again when he does feel that he has sinned. Dismiss him. You may want to have prayer first, however, thanking God "for this young child who is willing to do what is right." Make it easy for him to talk to you again, but do not continue. Do not say, "Oh, yes, you have too sinned!" and then name some. With children, wait for God's conviction.

d. If the answer is yes, continue. He may even give a personal illustration of some sin he has done recently or one that has bothered him.

e. Tell him what God says about sin: We've all sinned ("There is no one righteous, not even one," Rom. 3:10). And because of that sin, we can't get to God ("For the wages of sin is death . . . " Rom. 6:23). So He had to come to us (". . . but the gift of God is eternal life in Christ Jesus our Lord," Rom. 6:23).

    f. Relate God's gift of salvation to Christmas gifts-we don't earn them or pay for them; we just accept them and are thankful for them.

3. Bring the child to a definite decision.

    a. Christ must be received if salvation is to be possessed.

    b. Remember, do not force a decision.

    c. Ask the child to pray out loud in her own words. Give her some things she could say if she seems unsure. Now be prepared for a blessing! (It is best to avoid having the child repeat a memorized prayer after you. Let her think, and make it personal.)*

    d. After salvation has occurred, pray for her out loud. This is a good way to pronounce a blessing on her.

4. Lead your child into assurance. Show him that he will have to keep his relationship open with God through repentance and forgiveness (just like with his family or friends), but that God will always love him ("Never will I leave you; never will I forsake you," Heb. 13:5).

   * If you wish to guide your child through the prayer, here is some suggested language.

"Dear God, I know that I am a sinner [have child name specific sins he or she acknowledged earlier, such as lying, stealing, disobeying, etc.]. I know that Jesus died on the cross to pay for all my sins. I ask You to forgive me of my sins. I believe that Jesus died for me and rose from the dead, and I accept Him as my Savior. Thank You for loving me. In Jesus' name. Amen."

⭑ Endnotes ⭑

Introduction

1 Douglas Coupland, *Life after God* (New York: Pocket Books, 1994), 177-178.

2 Ibid., 178

Chapter 2

1 *The Bible Knowledge Commentary,* Eds. John F. Walvoord and Roy B. Zuck (Colorado Springs: Chariot Victor Books, 1985), 953.

Chapter 3

1 C.S. Lewis, *Mere Christianity* (New York: MacMillan Publishing Co., 1943), 39.

2 Allan Bloom, *The Closing of the American Mind* (New York: Simon and Schuster, 1987), 25-26.

Chapter 4

1 Dr. James Dobson, *Solid Answers* (Wheaton: Tyndale House, 1997), 216-217.

2 Douglas Wilson, *Recovering the Lost Tools of Learning* (Wheaton: Crossway Books, 1991), 92.

Chapter 6

1 C.S. Lewis, *Screwtape Letters* (New York: Bantam Books, 1982), xiii.

Chapter 8

1 C.S. Lewis, *God in the Dock* (Grand Rapids, MI: Eerdmans, 1970).

Chapter 14

1 M. Scott Peck, *The Road Less Traveled* (New York: Simon and Schuster, 1978), 19.

2 Ibid., 20.

3 Ibid.